S.H.E. Journey

[Seen It, Heard It, Experienced It]

Overcoming Life's
Challenges

Faylyn Kanneh

WESTBOW
PRESS®
A DIVISION OF THOMAS NELSON
& ZONDERVAN

This book is a work of non-fiction. Unless otherwise noted, the author and the publisher make no explicit guarantees as to the accuracy of the information contained in this book and in some cases, names of people and places have been altered to protect their privacy.

Unless otherwise indicated, scripture taken from the New King James Version®. Copyright © 1982 by Thomas Nelson. Used by permission. All rights reserved.

Scripture quotations marked (NIV) are taken from the Holy Bible, New International Version®, NIV®. Copyright © 1973, 1978, 1984, 2011 by Biblica, Inc.™ Used by permission of Zondervan. All rights reserved worldwide. www.zondervan.com The "NIV" and "New International Version" are trademarks registered in the United States Patent and Trademark Office by Biblica, Inc.™

Amplified Bible (AMP) Copyright © 1954, 1958, 1962, 1964, 1965, 1987 by The Lockman Foundation, La Habra, CA. All rights reserved. Used by Permission. www.lockman.org.

WestBow Press books may be ordered through booksellers or by contacting:

WestBow Press
A Division of Thomas Nelson & Zondervan
1663 Liberty Drive
Bloomington, IN 47403
www.westbowpress.com
1 (866) 928-1240

Because of the dynamic nature of the Internet, any web addresses or links contained in this book may have changed since publication and may no longer be valid. The views expressed in this work are solely those of the author and do not necessarily reflect the views of the publisher, and the publisher hereby disclaims any responsibility for them.

Any people depicted in stock imagery provided by Thinkstock are models, and such images are being used for illustrative purposes only.
Certain stock imagery © Thinkstock.

ISBN: 978-1-9736-0732-8 (sc)
ISBN: 978-1-9736-0731-1 (hc)
ISBN: 978-1-9736-0733-5 (e)

Library of Congress Control Number: 2017917640

Print information available on the last page.

WestBow Press rev. date: 11/21/2017

CONTENTS

ACKNOWLEDGMENTS

Special thanks to

John Graham, the senior pastor of Sovereign Ministries International London, who saw the potential in me to write this book. He encouraged me to write down the experiences I underwent during my journey.

Fiona Pottenger, a dear friend who started the journey with me and typed a few chapters to help me begin writing this book.

Errol Campbell my bishop from London, who believed in me when I first mentioned the idea about this book and encouraged me to move ahead.

Cherice Walford, who read my manuscript and helped in the proofreading process of this book.

Nicky M'Panzu, who also helped with some of the proofreading and wrote the foreword of the book.

Gloria Murray, who encouraged me not to give up on writing this book; she prayed with me and instilled confidence in me.

Serge M'Panzu worked tirelessly to design the cover of this book.

Lastly, and most importantly, my husband, **Charles**, who supported me on this journey. He introduced me to the publisher and worked with me through the night to complete the proofreading process of the entire book.

Everyone who said encouraging words one way or the other and prayed for me, I thank you. May God bless you richly.

FOREWORD

I'm glad and honored for the privilege I have to write the foreword for Fay's first book, in which she shares the experiences of her life's journey to wholeness. I'm sure this book will bless and encourage many people to find out who they really are, as a motivation to go ahead and be successful with great self-esteem.

Fay's journey has not only made her an authentic and sensitive person but also the bold preacher and teacher that she is today. Fay and I have been friends for the last sixteen years. As I recall parts of her journey, I laugh and sometimes cry. We studied together, served in Ministry together, and our families became interlinked. She is a godmother to one of my daughters.

The first time I met Miss Fay (as I usually call her) was when she came to our church, Alpha and Omega Christian Fellowship, at Kingsbury and London, United Kingdom. She was fairly new in England, and she gave her testimony. I can still hear her now. As she opened her mouth, it was as if she'd started to run off her résumé. She made quite an impact, and I knew she was someone who was going to make a mark.

This tall, attractive Jamaican young lady, who used to lead her choir back in Kingston, introduced herself and then sang, all in the space of a few minutes. This is how I would summarize it:

There are so many people who have no idea where they are heading and no idea of who they are or what their potential is. Therefore, live from day to day. "Que sera sera."

Often the route planned is influenced by the voiced opinions and comments of others. However, the day when truth is accepted, it points people in the right direction and awakens dormant dreams. We know this is the truth, as John 8:32 says, "Then you will know the truth, and the truth will set you free" (NIV). Yes, you will be free from the opinions of others and the lies of the enemy.

It was clear that Fay was at the beginning of a new journey in more ways than one. It was not just a new location, country, or adventure but a new journey of self-discovery.

It was not long before we were friends, and she became a part of our church worship team. Fay was clearly different from what we were used to. Her style, voice, sound, and attitude were all so distinctive. This at first, and for a long time, was a challenge. Despite all that, Fay forged through until she became needed, loved, and effectual. Was this easy? Not at all. This was not an overnight experience; it was years of comparisons, years of other people's opinions, and years of Fay's own negative opinions and inner struggles.

In 2012 we both became ordained ministers; this was a beautiful thing to have happen. It was a part of God's promise that we saw manifested. By this time she really had changed from who she used to be. Her confidence, boldness, gifting, and skills were so much sharper. Clearly, she just kept going from strength to strength. Her relationship with Jesus is one to be admired; it challenges people to press in deeper.

Fay's life really is one that has had many hill-and-valley experiences. There have been so many tears as she battled with physical, financial, emotional, and psychological challenges, doubts, and bouts of anxiety and depression. As I write this, I think back and say, "Wow."

So many prophetic words spoken over her through the years made clear to her that God saw and knew. He was going to see her through her change, as He had great plans for her. This woman had location changes, friend changes, educational changes, health changes, employment changes, changes in skill sets and mindset, and more.

I'll just share this last insight regarding her journey. Before returning to Jamaica and later on moving to America and becoming a Mrs., Fay enrolled to participate in a Christian counselling course that I was teaching. It is a course that leads to a qualification in counselling. While on this course, it happened to many, including me, that we were revealed to ourselves and the Father's unique design for us. This started to give language to Fay about who she was. It started to expose things, give reasons for responses and patterns, and make her aware of potential trouble spots. The bible scriptures became new also her for her journey, temperament, and relationships. Her vision changed because of the clarity about who she was. Our relationship became precious, and the unspoken, unaddressed underlying tensions between us were broken.

This is important to know: we were friends, good friends—that was never in doubt. However, there was much that got in the way. Once we came into knowledge of who we were, it changed everything.

Philippians 1:6 tells us, "Being confident of this, that He who began a good work in you is faithful to bring it to completion."

Our friendship continues, and we have become as close as sisters. I wish that Fay were still in England, as I miss her so much. However, I believe that God allowed her to move on because He has a purpose for His children in every situation, as the scripture says in Romans 8:28: "And we know that all things work together for good to them that love God, to them who are the called according to his purpose."

Nicky M'Panzu
Pastor, teacher, counselor, and friend

PREFACE

I believe the idea of writing this book was given to me by God. I was to deliver a message to those who have found themselves in a rut for years and are trying to use their own solutions to escape the struggles of life. Since this subject is so personal to me, I assure you that I have seen, heard, and experienced many tough situations. I can truly say that if the Lord had not been on my side, I would have been cast out.

Being a dedicated Christian takes much more than just going to church and reading the word of God. It's about having a relationship with the creator and understanding who you are and whose you are. The process can be difficult at first, but when you know that God is on your side it makes a big difference. According to Jeremiah 29:11, "He knows the thoughts He thinks towards you."

The best is yet to come for you; it takes patience and endurance to win the race. God placed this book (*S.H.E. Journey*) in my spirit years ago, and I was inspired by the Holy Spirit to share with others the road from then to now. It wasn't easy. Many times I tried giving up and telling myself that I couldn't, but I encouraged myself in the Lord.

I can clearly remember when I shared my vision with a dear friend, Pastor John Graham. He encouraged me to move forward with what God had deposited in me. I struggled for many years to complete this book, finding many excuses not to proceed. I thank God for Gloria, who for some reason I got connected with when I arrived in the United States. Through the Holy Spirit she inspired me and encouraged me to continue with my book project. She thought it was a very important message for others out there, so I again took up the writing until it was completed.

God will set you up for greatness if you abide in His will and purpose to serve Him. My husband, family, and friends have provided consistent encouragement to me and prayed for this book to have a special value to the kingdom of God. You may believe that there is no way out of your situation, but as you read this book you will realize that God still works miracles, and He always answers on time. I give all the glory to God for the positive effect I believe *S.H.E. Journey* will have on the lives of all those who read it.

INTRODUCTION

In my Christian life I have observed that God doesn't waste anything. He uses everything and all our experiences to help us through our journeys. Everything happens in our lives for a reason, and a great part of that reason is to help us grow in our faith—especially when we are baptized with the Holy Ghost and fire. It has been said that life has to be lived in a forward motion; however it can only be understood by looking back and taking note of ourselves through a microscope. This would outline every detail of our life cycles and allow us to know who we really are.

This demands that we trust in the loving purposes of a sovereign God who knows our every move and each detail about us. We must trust that He is in full control of our developmental areas of life, which include our physical, emotional, and spiritual beings. When life seems to be out of control for us, He has already said:

> "I know the thoughts that I think towards
> you," says the Lord, "thoughts of peace and
> not of evil, to give you a future and a hope."
> —Jeremiah 29:11

Such was the life of the Old Testament characters, some of the women and men I will mention in this book. Their lives were filled with dark and difficult experiences, yet their final outcomes are recorded as amazing and mind-blowing. They were all determined to overcome the challenges of life, using the unction and direction of God through His word.

These individuals and their life cycles teach us how to deal with our entangled lives and how to be patient in the waiting process. Their examples can help us as we face the issues of life and begin to develop momentum in our endeavors.

God knew every detail about these individuals' lives, and He knows every detail about our lives.

It's a privilege to partner with God, exploring who He has called us to be and what He has called us to do as we celebrate life together.

PART I

CHAPTER 1

KNOWING WHO YOU ARE

We have been created and fashioned in the image of God. We were created with the ability to reflect His character in the way we love. This is extended into patience, faithfulness, kindness, and other fruit-bearing traits. We are created to be the image of the heavenly Father, our creator, and he named us mankind, who we were formed to be.

> He created them male and female, and
> blessed them and called them Mankind
> in the day they were created.
> —Genesis 5:2

Therefore man was created by God and given a name, Adam. This name represents who he is and who he was called to become on the earth. Remember that Adam was given dominion and authority. He was the one in perfect fellowship with the Father. He was presented with animals, and he named them. Names are very important in our lives, for our callings and destinies.

When I was born, my parents decided what I would respond to. Our names carry weight, and mine highlights some of my personality traits: my character, desires, ideals, goals, ambitions, and also my potential. When I was a young girl growing up, that name became a part of my destiny.

Whether or not I liked the name, I didn't have a choice in the matter; I carried that name. It meant who I was—what it said, and what it represented—each time someone declared my name.

As time went by, I matured in life and began to understand the importance of names. In all honesty, I didn't like my name because of the sound of the syllables it contains. The struggle I had was that my name sounded like *failing* rather than Faylyn. The thought of being a failure and the fact that I was failing in some areas of my life gave me an urge to change my name.

At college I had a lecturer who asked the class members to introduce themselves by standing and giving their names. When it was my turn, I stood up and said, "My name is Faylyn."

As I sat down, the lecturer declared with a cheeky grin on his face, "I will not be calling you *failing*, but I will call you *success* instead." I remember this so vividly. I didn't know whether he was joking or not, but I somehow took it the wrong way, and from then on it plagued my mind.

I wasn't impressed with his statement. I just suppressed my feelings, as I usually did, and received the words that he had spoken to me with a heavy heart and a fake smile. Was I clear about whom I was at that particular time in that classroom? No! Even though the lecturer didn't say that I was failing or that I was a failure, I accepted the negative and allowed it to play an active role in my life for a long time. This is what the enemy Satan will do to us as Christians. He will cause us to accept the negative words that have been spoken over our lives and allow it to refuse what God has said about us— who we are when we came to know Him as our Lord and Savior.

Name-calling is in fact a serious thing. We can quite easily be misrepresented, misunderstood, and confused about who we are. It's important for us to know the truth, and it will certainly put our minds at ease and set us free.

Faylyn means "faith" and "a noble friend with good leadership qualities." It also means someone who is gifted with creative ideas and who will endeavor to implement them. It also implies discerning and inspiring qualities.

> And you shall know the truth, and
> the truth shall make you free.
> —John 8:32

When we know what the truth is, we will eventually accept freedom and change. We will be able to become bold in whatever our passions and destinies are. The truth also enables us to be honest with ourselves and boldly appreciate who we represent, not try to imitate others. When we are free, we can demonstrate our true selves. The lies of the enemy and imagination once held me bound to believe I was a failure rather than accepting the declaration that I'm a leader. May we truly know who we are and recognize the one who called us to be the persons we are meant to be.

What is your identity?

Years ago I worked as a pharmacist's assistant in Jamaica. Even though I wasn't a pharmacist by profession, I was carrying out the duties of a pharmacist. I operated like this for over seven years, filling prescriptions and recommending medication to the patients who did not have a prescription but wanted over-the-counter drugs. I was also administering pregnancy tests and blood tests.

I knew that I was not a pharmacist; however, when I was called a pharmacist by customers and by friends, I straightaway answered to that identity. I didn't correct the customers at the counter to let them know that I was just assisting the pharmacist as I carried out the same duties. I was very good at my job, and the training I had received over the years allowed me to become an expert. I walked in the shadow of a pharmacist without the proper qualifications and hard work that professional pharmacists undergo while studying for their degrees.

The simple reason was that I wanted to be known and identified as someone special within that field. I refused to accept and make known the truth about myself. I had very low self-esteem, inadequate feelings about myself, and I wanted to fit in. This made me take on someone else's identity, to make myself be known and not feel left out. I was more worried about what other people thought of me than about my personal attributes and feelings. I didn't know who I was; therefore I relied on public opinion to judge my value.

These kinds of behaviors happen all the time all over the world. When we don't know who we are, we need the right people, those with a passion for God, around us. They will support, develop, and educate us through the word of God to become who we are. Jesus left us the perfect template to prevent us from copying and allow us to walk in our uniqueness. God wants to meet us at the point where we feel lost in ourselves and unable to identify who it is He has created in His own image and likeness.

God knows us, and He knows who we are from the time before we were created. Over and over again, we want to be like others. We hide ourselves from the truth of who we really are—our self-image, our true personality.

We do not have to accept what people say about us, whether it is to make us feel good or bad. The important thing is that as individuals we need to know who we are. Then we will be able to find the right jobs, marry the right persons, and communicate effectively, without self-pity and low self-esteem.

When we are honest with ourselves and conduct a thorough search to know the truth, we will be truly unique and not carbon copies of someone else.

CHAPTER 2

REMOVING THE MASK

> But we all, with unveiled face, beholding as
> in a mirror the glory of the Lord, are being
> transformed into the same image from glory
> to glory, just as by the Spirit of the Lord.
> —2 Corinthians 3:18

For a season I lived in London, and it gave me many opportunities. I was a co-leader of an anointed worship team, and there were various opportunities to visit and minister. There was a high level of vulnerability and openness to function effectively in the team. It was our continuous desire to seek and do what the Lord wanted us to when we all came together. Here I could not pretend or play or take on a role but experienced the first desire to be open with the Father and successfully lead in worship.

In the book of John 1, John the Baptist refused to wear a mask because he wanted to be identified as himself. Many people today are walking around with someone else's identity. They are wearing masks that don't quite fit their true image. The masks disguise who they truly are and cause a serious effect that may develop later on into isolation.

The effect could also develop further into a false identity that becomes a shield. Not achieving a true identity could result in emotional damage and brokenheartedness because of counterfeit personality.

It is important to know the truth about ourselves and the name each of us portrays within society. Furthermore, we should honestly take surveys of our lives, both current and past, to be ready for healthy relationships in the future.

Our Father knows the truth, and when we come into agreement, He will position us for freedom and success.

> However, when He, the spirit of truth, has
> come, He will guide you into all truth; for
> He will not speak on his own authority,
> but whatever He hears He will speak;
> and He will tell you things to come.
> —John 16:13

Knowing the truth about what Jesus says to us and about us is vital. Jesus Christ said to His disciples, "I will go and when I go I will send the Holy Spirit, (the comforter) the one who will reveal the truth to us about ourselves according to the word of God."

Now, people will say things about you that are not necessarily the things your true character represents. It is important whether you accept what they say about you or refuse it. John clearly spoke the truth about who he really was, and he became free—and free from the public opinion in regards to his life.

Once they had finished telling John who they thought he was, they finally gave up and instead asked him, "Who are you?" They became persistent to receive an answer—the truth. John was on a mission, a journey. He became visible to others. He was called, and he was separated, and therefore individuals would enquire about his true identity.

Then they said to him, "Who are you, that
we may give an answer to those who sent
us? What do you say about yourself?"

—John 1:22

What do you really know about yourself? If you were asked
this question, what would your response be? Would your answer
come from among those below?

- Your current position
- Public opinion
- Fears or insecurities
- Someone else's identity
- The person God called you to be

The truth is that we disguise ourselves with masks because
of past experiences. We find it difficult to accept who we are; we
struggle in not knowing who we are. We don't know what we are
capable of or the destiny, plan, or purpose we find ourselves aligned
with. We could be in the wrong job or the wrong relationship.

Now is the time to seek and find the truth by removing the
masks or protective walls that we have built around ourselves. A
woman in natural labor cannot give birth with her legs closed. It is
time to press into what heaven is saying *about* and *for* each of us.

CHAPTER 3

WHO YOU REALLY ARE

What are God's thoughts for us? Is it important? What is the point of pursuing destiny without knowing who we are?

> "I know the thoughts that I think towards you," says the Lord, "thoughts of peace and not of evil, to give you a future and a hope."
> —Jeremiah 29:11

God wants to transform and bring us into the position to fulfill His purpose. He is calling us to change, purpose, transformation, and freedom. Many people are walking hopeless, helpless, and ready to give up on life.

We run to various avenues as we seek help to erase or numb the pain and hurt. General recommendations usually are to go on holiday or sabbatical or to seek medical assistance. Sometimes the answers to our questions are not clear; it is at this stage that we need to dig deeper and be persistent in our search for direction. The assistance of wise counsel would be of great value in reaching to the place of freedom, through God's word, toward our destiny.

My people are destroyed for lack of knowledge.
Because you have rejected knowledge, I also
will reject you from being priest for me;
because you have forgotten the law of your
God, I also will forget your children.

—Hosea 4:6

God wants to change our names and identify us as His children. God has marked us for a purpose, not to be destroyed and tossed aside. His mark upon us brings us out of bondage and places us before great men; this positions us in His perfect will.

We have been taught and pressured by society to believe that success comes from our accomplishments: jobs, marital status, and titles we may hold. All of our worldly fame means nothing if we haven't come into the knowledge of who we are and whose we are. Thus, when you are chosen by God, He will totally disregard your accomplishments and all the things individuals honor you for.

He will then transform you and make you His, to serve Him faithfully and righteously and to pursue His will for your life until He returns.

But you are a chosen generation, a royal
priesthood, a Holy nation, His own
special people, that you may proclaim
the praises of Him who called you out of
darkness into His marvelous light,
Who once were not a people but are now
the people of God, who had not obtained
mercy but now have obtained mercy.

—1 Peter 2:9–10

Let's look again at John the Baptist and his interaction when people asked him who he was. He expressed the leadership skills and behavior traits that reminded and pointed the crowd to Elijah and Jesus. That was very high praise, but that wasn't what John was or the job he was supposed to do. He was different; he was John the Baptist the one called to make the way straight for the coming King.

We should be like John, getting to know who we are and proclaiming it. It might be a compliment for others to reference you as some other great leader but always remember God has called you specifically to do something, especially in a particular time. Then John replied not by what others called him or thought he was but by the name God gave to Him.

> He said: "I am The voice of one calling in
> the wilderness: 'Make straight the way for
> the Lord,' as the prophet Isaiah said."
> —John 1:23

What are we called to do?

Frequently as we go through our childhood and adolescent years, one of the most frequently and most used questions is what we will become when we grow up. Sometimes, we choose based on circumstances, household expectations or pressures or what seems easiest at the time.

There is predestination on our lives. God has called some of us to be role models, a mentor, a leader, a teacher, an apostle, a prophet, an evangelist, a pastor, and the list goes on. Therefore, whoever God has called us to be He will reveal it to us as we seek His face.

I've been through the same process. I've always thought of who I wanted to become, and my environment impacted my thought process.

Who am I? What am I good at? What does my character say about me? Why do I want to launch into this thing? These were some of the general thoughts I had when trying to process my identity.

What is identity; and how does it relate to destiny? Dictionary. com describes Identity as a condition or character as to who a person or what a thing is; the qualities, beliefs, etc., that distinguish or identify a person or thing. Each individual is unique; our fingerprints are different.

Each one of us was created uniquely. God said we are fearfully and wonderfully made. In fact, even our very finger prints are not duplicated.

> I will praise You, for I am fearfully
> and wonderfully made;
> Marvelous are Your works,
> And that my soul knows very well.
> —Psalm 139:14

Are you still searching for your identity or accepting what people think or say about you? The question still remains, who are you?

You will find your answer in Christ; He is the one who will truly make the difference. In my own experience, my need for value and affirmation became urgent the more intimate I was with my heavenly Father. As a matter of fact, the world encourages us to acquire everything for ourselves and our own personal wealth development.

Our identity issues started in the garden. Because of sin we lost who we were created to be. Even though we were born in sin and shaped in iniquity, through the shed blood of Jesus we have the opportunity to be transformed and renewed. We now have a hope; we can now leave the state of hopelessness and be transformed into His image.

Does it mean that because I was in sin or because I'm a sinner, I don't know who I am? No! There are people who are very confident about who they are and what they desire in life. It doesn't signify that they have got it all accurate or that they have made the right choices. We are all capable of making wrong decisions and preferences. We fail in our past and present life and some of us are still failing because of adoptions in our lifestyles.

As the word of God clearly states:

> "For all have sinned and fall
> short of the glory of God."
>
> —Romans 3:23

CHAPTER 4

THE CHOICES YOU MAKE

> My little children, these things I write
> to you, so that you may not sin. And if
> anyone sins, we have an Advocate with
> the Father, Jesus Christ the righteous.
>
> —1 John 2:1

The story of David is very popular. He was called a man after God's own heart. As much as David loved God, he made some wrong choices in his life, which caused him to sin against Him.

Was that because he didn't know who he was? He made a wrong choice that blindfolded his identity in God and caused him to sin against his creator. He separated himself from who he was and went on to pursue the lustful desire of his nature.

God chose David for a purpose. He selected him to become the king of Israel, to govern the land and lead his people, because his predecessors had failed. David sinned, not because he was a king but because he made a wrong decision and followed the path of immorality, which many of us are still doing today.

When David came to a place of truth and remembered who he truly was, he turned his heart to God and pleaded for mercy with sincere heart, mind, and soul. David was anointed for a purpose;

there was no escape for him. He had to submit totally to the will of God.

> Behold, I was brought forth in iniquity,
> And in sin my mother conceived me.
> Behold, You desire truth in the inward parts,
> And in the hidden part You will
> make me to know wisdom.
> —Psalm 51:5–6

David remembered who he was and repented right away. Then he turned and asked for cleansing and restoration. God wants us to identify with the place we are in our walks and the purpose in our hearts to become who he wants us to be. We do not need to remain in sinful states or linger in the lifestyle that we are in.

We should aim to be like David, coming to our Father in honest repentance. God wants transformation to take action in our natural and spiritual lives. He longs for us to become better individuals. He is seeking for us to know who we are in Him—to be set apart, holy, and free from the sins of this world. By this we will procure the things of God and make the accurate choices for our lives.

Choices are very important, and it's essential to make the right ones. Now we can choose whether to remain in our current state or to indicate whether we are even ready. What we need to do is change the way we think—and then act.

My journey took me in so many directions. I was still perplexed about who I wanted to become as an adult. I tried to fit myself in so many different things, but nothing that I tried would connect. It felt as if I were trying to fit a jigsaw puzzle piece in position and choosing the wrong piece all the time. For example, my journey in the pharmacy lasted over seven years. I then decided to continue my education in business and computer studies.

The choices I made were not from knowing who I was and what I wanted to do. I was confused and making wrong choices. I realized that making incorrect choices was causing me to lose my dignity and self-esteem. It was bringing major delays into my life and leaving me even more confused and helpless.

Hopelessness became my state of being. I went to others, seeking my identity in what they could tell me. I went to the wrong sources; my choice was among man and not God. He is the one who knows all things, from the foundation of the earth, from the beginning to the end. It was decision time, and for that reason I sought out the Lord for His divine help and intervention. I was then led to something that would not have crossed my mind otherwise. If someone had told me that caring for children would be the starting point of my work, I would have accused the person of making up stories.

CHAPTER 5

GOD'S PLANS FOR OUR LIVES

I remember that as a teenager, growing up and being among my siblings, I cared for my nieces and nephews. I remember being told that I didn't know how to care for children. "You're too harsh with them," people said. I accepted all that was said about me with a hard heart and a smile pasted on my face, and I moved on with life.

There came a time when I intentionally sought a period of reflection to look at bad words spoken over me. I recognized that it was time for me to renounce all the negative words and replace them in a positive way—by believing and declaring the truth about myself. This was my fresh start. The Lord brought a scripture back to me, and it became a life source which I've held onto until this very day.

> "For My thoughts are not your thoughts, Nor
> are your ways My ways," says the Lord.
> —Isaiah 55:8

The truth of this quotation has become a mantle for me. I use it in every situation that is difficult for me to handle on my own. I recite it until it becomes my secret weapon.

As we continue to learn from our choices, we realize that they help us to identify who we are as individuals. They further teach us whether we are in the wrong or walking the right path. When we choose to know Christ and accept Him as our Lord and Savior, along with His guidance, we experience a change in our lives and a freshness in Him.

Like a new birth, your identity will be different. Your character and will power will eventually start changing course and heading for a total transformation.

> Therefore, if anyone is in Christ, he is a
> new creation; old things have passed away;
> behold, all things have become new.
> —2 Corinthians 5:17

New birth is occurring because we have made a choice, a choice to accept the truth. The choice is to accept Jesus Christ as the one who will make the difference in our lives and to become a better person in Him. He will rearrange our lives, adjust our personalities, and enable us to experience the covenant of peace as promised.

When you accept the Lord Jesus as your Savior, does it really help me to know who you are? Does it actually take away all the lack of enthusiasm you feel toward yourself? Does it give you a satisfying relief to the torture of self-pity? The answer is yes! God wants to show you and teach you everything that will help you know who you are and what he wants you to become. He wants you to be His friend, and He wants to direct your path and order your steps in knowing who you are through His word.

> No longer do I call you servants, for a
> servant does not know what his master
> is doing; but I have called you friends,
> for all things that I heard from my
> Father I have made known to you.
> —John 15:15

Without the friendship of God, our minds become trapped in slave mentality. We become victims of our environment. God said He wants to become our companion and associate in order to change the slavery mentality and direct us in the freedom of knowing who we are. This will transform our way of thinking and attitude toward life, as scripture tells us in Romans.

> But now having been set free from sin, and
> having become slaves of God, you have your
> fruit to holiness, and the end, everlasting life.
> —Romans 6:22

This is what God did for me. He brought me to a place where I started to regard my life differently. I began to think positively about myself even though there were still stacks and layers of certain situations surrounding me and causing delays in my life cycle. I continued to encourage myself through the process of renovation.

This is exactly what David did in the bible. The word of God tells us that he encouraged himself in the Lord. This helped him to overcome the obstacles and pressures of life that he faced when he returned home to find everything had been destroyed and taken away from him. He faced a great ordeal and it seemed that all was against him. He was in a distressed state, and the feeling of grief and pain overwhelmed him.

David was troubled and in pain. The reaction of the soldiers who were fighting along with him was not the kind of response he wanted. They were very angry; they wanted to stone him. They thought of violence in their time of distress and sorrow, but David encouraged himself in the Lord. The Lord was his source, his anchor, and the one who knew about his pain.

> Now David was greatly distressed, for the
> people spoke of stoning him, because the
> soul of all the people was grieved, every man
> for his sons and his daughters. But David
> strengthened himself in the LORD his God.
>
> —1 Samuel 30:6

How often do we actually encourage ourselves in the Lord when we face troubles—when we are distressed, misjudged, belittled, and put down? It's a very difficult thing to do, but it can be done. David had personal experience with God, so he trusted Him to be his deliverer from the situation he was facing.

I was given the opportunity to work with children even though it had been declared earlier in my life that I would not do right by them. This came about because I had to work to pay the bills, and my thoughts were on who I was and what God was calling me to be.

I was a single woman living away from family, and they were not in a position to support me financially. My contract had expired, and I had been unemployed for approximately two months. I had a friend I was helping by cooking her personal meals, since at that time she wasn't able to do it by herself.

As she was aware of my situation, she introduced me to a friend of hers who owned a nursery. This was set up by God—the friend needed a cook for the nursery. I was interviewed, was given the post, and almost immediately began working as a part-time cook. It wasn't long before I was given the role on a full-time basis, as they were extremely pleased with my work.

My appetite was whet, and I knew right away I had the potential to do better. Being in the nursery environment reawakened my desire to work among children, as well as to go back and study. Yes, finally I was holding the correct jigsaw puzzle piece before me. It felt right, so I decided to enquire about the different courses that could lead me into the role of a nursery teacher.

Unbeknown to me, I was being watched by my manager, and she also was drawn to the potential in me. I had already started on the journey of encouraging myself, and now someone on the outside was partnering in the encouragement. I will always be grateful to her, as she helped me to get started and inspired me to pursue the courses.

In my first interview for the course I was to choose the option of level 2 or level 3 in child care. During the process of the interview, the woman decided to place me in the higher-level course. She said to me, "You are qualified for level 3 because you have the ability to accomplish it."

After the interview that day, I was motivated to pursue further. Uh-oh! My proprietor was not happy. She wanted me to remain in the kitchen, but my manager insisted that I move forward with the courses.

I worked in the kitchen for approximately six months and also was allowed the opportunity to work with the children. After the six months, I was promoted to work with the children on a full-time basis. Six months later I received my level 3 certificate in child care. If I hadn't made the choice to serve in the kitchen behind the scenes, it would have taken a lot longer for me to get on track in my journey.

This happened because I refused to accept what people said about me. I knew what I wanted, and I was learning at the same time about who I was. The process wasn't easy. I faced obstacles, and at times I felt like giving up. There were people who came into my life to encourage me and others who remained to be thorns in my flesh, but nevertheless I persevered.

I remember days when I was in the pit of despair. Instead of spending time with God and asking him what to do, I did stupid things that I was not able to learn from. I was hurting, and so I hurt others around me. The saying "Hurting people hurt people" is true. During the pain and the hurt I built walls around myself, and it took the power and mercy of God for me to come into agreement with heaven to tear them down.

When criticism came, I decided to build walls of defense to protect myself from being hurt. During this time I gave room to the enemy to enter my life, and now I thought that the whole world was against me. I thought I had no friends, that everyone saw me as weird and self-centered. I struggled with my imagination, and this fortified my need for protection.

In defending myself, I was firing darts at other people—even the ones who genuinely cared about me. I justified it by saying I was protecting myself. I took matters into my own hands and pushed people away, but there were some desperate cries for help from inside.

You may be in a situation in which you can't see the consequences of wrong decisions. You need to seek help beyond the walls of protecting yourself. When trouble comes, do not be too quick to respond or retaliate.

CHAPTER 6

IT'S NOT IMPOSSIBLE

When God visited Abram and Sarai, He had a plan and a purpose for them. In order for the plan and purpose to be fulfilled in them, He had to change their names.

Abram was changed to Abraham and Sarai to Sarah. Their destiny could not be fulfilled until their names were changed to represent the calling on their lives. Abram did not know who he was; God had to visit him in a vision, and then He rewarded him for his faithfulness.

Abram was still questioning and reminding God about his status at the time. There are points in our lives when we ask God about our lives yet on the other hand we want to tell God what to do because of the situation. The Lord took Abram out of his situation and showed him what was promised to him.

The extension of Abram's seed was without number, and because of that God told him that he would no longer be called Abram but Abraham, "For I have made thee a father of many nations" (Genesis 17:4). *Wow!* It didn't stop there. God said that He would make him exceedingly fruitful, and God also made a covenant with mankind. He wanted to transform us and set us free to do His will.

Sarai's name was also changed, to Sarah. In Sarai's case, she doubted God. She laughed at the promise God made that she would bear a child at the age of ninety years.

And I will bless her and also give you
a son by her; then I will bless her, and
she shall be a mother of nations; kings
of peoples shall be from her.
Then Abraham fell on his face and laughed,
and said in his heart, "Shall a child be born to
a man who is one hundred years old? And shall
Sarah, who is ninety years old, bear a child?"

—Genesis 17:16–17

Have you ever been in a situation as impossible as Sarah's and thought there was no hope? Well, can you just imagine how Sarah felt when God told her she would have a child? We often face the hardship of choosing whether to trust someone else or ourselves.

When someone says that they don't trust themselves, does that mean they are unaware of who they are or what they are capable of achieving? Well, yes—when we rely on someone to do something for us or to honor their word, and they don't follow through, we tend to lose trust in what they say.

Sarah had a history of mistrust with her handmaid Hagar. That lack of trust grew within her until she didn't care who it was; she would not believe or be open to any more promises. But it is important to believe that God can heal you. He will deliver you from that lack of trust and give you the freedom of hope and faith.

I remember that years back I had an experience at a sale outlet. There were some men selling stereos for a reasonable price. At the time I was desperate for a stereo, and I wanted to get one at a reasonable cost.

A leaflet was dropped at my house advertising this sale, and I got really excited when I realized that the prices were good. The auction started and the bids began. I quickly threw my hand up, as everyone was so eager to get their stereos. When I got to the front of the queue and collected my stereo, it was in a nice box and looking really brand new.

I took this risk because I believed the deal was genuine. Every time my mind wanders back, I think of how naive I was to make that decision. I took the stereo home and was so excited to unwrap it. To my surprise, the stereo was all covered in rust, and it could not function. I had been deceived. It was a difficult lesson to learn, and this scenario tarnished my trust for any sale outlets.

There could be other circumstances in which you have been deceived: in relationships, family matters, church situations, or other circumstances. In the areas that we have experienced lack of trust, God can heal us through His word if we only believe. Lack of faith can lead to not trusting God's word.

Sarah did not believe that she could bear a child at the age of ninety years; hence she laughed and doubted what God had said. The situation might be difficult, but God can. Here's what he said in His word, making reference to Abraham and Sarah's situation:

> "Is anything too hard for the LORD? At the
> appointed time I will return to you, according
> to the time of life, and Sarah shall have a son."
> —Genesis 18:14

There is nothing too difficult for God to do in our lives. God wants to change things for us. He wants to help us find out who we are and work with what we have. We are not limited, we are bountiful; we are not failures, we were born to succeed; we are not below average, we walk in excellence; we are not stressed, we have peace; we are not poor, we are rich in Christ; we are not unstable, we are balanced; we are not beggars, we are a source of provision; we are not what people say we are; we are what God says we are. We are special; we are fearfully and wonderfully made. We are the head and not the tail. We are a royal priesthood, that's who we are, when we are in Him.

For there is not a word on my tongue, But
behold, O Lord, You know it altogether.

—Psalm 139:4

God has set us apart for a purpose, and He will not leave us
nor forsake us. He is the God that fulfils His promises and not
a man, that He should lie. He chose us, called us by name, and
placed us on a pedestal. God wants to show us off, and that's why
He called us His own.

But you are a chosen generation, a royal
priesthood, a holy nation, His own special
people, that you may proclaim the praises of
Him who called you out of darkness into His
marvelous light; who once were not a people
but are now the people of God, who had not
obtained mercy but now have obtained mercy.

—1 Peter 2:9-10

God made that covenant with Abraham for a reason, and for
that reason we are still partakers of His promise if we are faithful.
As believers we need to obey His word and keep His covenant.
Abraham kept His covenant. Even though his faith was tested,
he continued to trust in God totally for the impossible—for what
seems impossible to man is possible to God.

Do you believe in God for a miracle? Do you have a situation
in which doubt has stifled your belief in God's word? I challenge
you today, as you read this book, to take a moment and ask God
to take over your situation and lighten your burdens. Let them
go! Pour out before him in your word, and let Him know exactly
how you feel right now. Then wait for Him to speak to you. He is
right there with you, so just give it all to Him. He will make your
crooked path straight and lighten your burdens.

I will bring the blind by a way
they did not know;
I will lead them in paths they have not known.
I will make darkness light before them,
and crooked places straight.
These things I will do for them,
And not forsake them.

—Isaiah 42:16

That is what God has promised. His word will not return unto Him void but will accomplish what He set out to do. Therefore, in the process of knowing who we are, let us start by giving up certain habits and traits and following the right path. Let us stop pleasing people and instead please God. Let us stop doubting ourselves and instead trust God. Let us lay aside the negative thinking and start being positive in our minds. Let us cast away all fear of failure and allow the nature of success to take its position in us.

Let us stop criticizing ourselves and instead speak promise over our lives. If we are tempted to say no to the will of God, instead we should say yes. Finally, let us stop procrastinating and move forward into our destiny and the calling of God on our lives.

So shall My word be that goes
forth from My mouth;
It shall not return to Me void,
But it shall accomplish what I please,
And it shall prosper in the
thing for which I sent it.

—Isaiah 55:11

Believe it, receive it, and run with it.

Ask God to show you who you truly are in Him, and follow His direction.

PART II

CHAPTER 7

HAVING A MADE-UP MIND

For all the promises of God in Him are Yes, and
in Him Amen, to the glory of God through us.
—2 Corinthians 1:20

There is an old saying that goes, "You have to stand for something
or you will fall for everything." There was a significant moment
in my life when I had to make a decision completely committed
to the call. There was a young man who drew my affection. At
that time I wasn't sure whether I wanted to stay in church or not.

I was still taking active roles in church and was very uncomfortable
playing the part. I was in an unsuitable position, and I decided to
strengthen my feelings toward this guy instead of following the
Christian path. I didn't show much interest in church anymore.

I attended church occasionally and had a planned excuse for
my spiritual leaders whenever I saw them. I was an active member
of the worship team, and I felt that I wasn't needed at times. My
space was already being filled by someone else. I was walking
contrary to the word of God. This guy I'd met would invite me out
on weekends and during the week. I used to sacrifice my Sundays
for this guy, meeting his families.

We became good friends, and we were having fun. That's
what I thought fun was for me—not totally following the

commandments of God. It happened that every time I attended church and had a conversation with my friend, he would say that my behavior and language toward him were changing.

I became frustrated with his comments each time we met. My feelings toward him were now different, and I became uncomfortable with him. While attending a church meeting with a few friends, I was convicted by the message that was preached. I went home that night and wept bitterly. I realized that I wasn't at the place where God wanted me to be. I had to make a decision between God and that guy.

Even though I was unfaithful to God in trying to satisfy my own desires, God was still knocking on the door of my heart to get me to surrender all to Him. The relationship between me and this guy was on the verge of breaking up. I cared very much for this young man and wanted our relationship to go further. But the Lord spoke to me, and I decided to end the relationship with him.

My mind was made up concerning who I wanted in my life. There was a strong force that kept pulling me in the opposite direction of the Lord's command. I then decided to give in, and I finally faced the truth about the one who makes the difference in my life—the one who keeps me going, the one who turns my morning into dancing and gives me peace (Jesus). After making the decision, I carried on building back my relationship with God. It has not been easy, but I have persevered.

I thought I was fully recovering and on my way to the right path. Then came a shock: I was tempted to go back into the trap of the enemy. However, I was reminded of the faithfulness of God. He loves us so much and never fails. He will not change His mind and will not go back on His word.

Making a decision is not an easy thing to do. It takes a made-up mind and a commitment to make a choice.

Many people find it difficult to make decisions, whether these involve work, church, or home situations.

In some cultures it happens that a father chooses for his daughter a suitable man to become her husband. His choice would be final.

A woman might go into a shoe store and see a wide selection of shoes to choose from. This woman has to make up her mind which pair she will take with her when she completes her shopping for the day.

God has given us a choice between heaven and hell. We must choose which to serve. Coming to Jesus Christ does not happen by force; it's a choice. We must have our minds made up. There are people who really don't know about Jesus and His saving grace. Many of God's followers were either invited by someone, or had a dream or vision by the Holy Spirit, or knew someone who was serving Him and then opted to make a decision. Whatever the case, God wants us to be in relationship with Him. He wants to love us and give us rewards and blessings.

Life does not always turn out the way we want it to; there are challenges along the way. We can choose what we want to move on in life—making the right decision or staying in the situation and being stifled.

There is a well-known story in the Bible about a woman called Ruth. She was a destitute widow who lost her husband and was about to lose her mother-in-law. Now, there are some people who would not mind losing their mothers-in-law, because they are not always easygoing (especially when it has anything to do with their sons). However, this case was different.

Naomi, the mother-in-law of Ruth, was a woman of dignity, strength, and character. She maintained her word even though she had also lost her husband as well as her two sons.

The remarkable thing about these two women was that they had a strong bond between them. Ruth saw something rewarding in her mother in law and aimed to achieve whatever she had to offer, even though Naomi said she had nothing left to offer. Ruth didn't let go, because she perceived greatness and wisdom that she wanted to be a part of.

The story is told in Ruth 1:1–10.

Your situation might not be the same as that of Ruth and Naomi. You may have lost family members and relationships, or you may have suffered a divorce or be heading in that direction. Not all situations can be controlled the same way, but once you've decided to place your situation in the hands of the one who can—God—He will make a difference in your life.

Listening to what people say, in some cases, may not be the best way forward. There are individuals who will give the wrong advice, which will cause us to miss opportunities of rescue. We ought to be mindful of who we decide to follow. We must know the direction they are heading and their purpose. There are people who are leaders but are not necessarily called to lead. Therefore, we should be careful to follow their instructions in order not to divert ourselves into situations of pain and sorrow. God should be at the forefront of our lives, and it is essential that we are led by the Spirit. God requests that we put our complete confidence in Him, as He directs us.

It is so easy to fall back into the trap of the enemy, but we need to know who we are and who we belong to. You may be in a relationship at present and feel that it's all you have. You may feel that if you lose it you will have nothing. The devil is a liar. God has so much more in store for you. We change our minds so many times and become vulnerable and helpless because of our situations. God wants to rescue us and give us peace. We just need to let go and let God.

> But those who wait on the LORD
> Shall renew their strength;
> They shall mount up with wings like eagles,
> They shall run and not be weary,
> They shall walk and not faint.
> —Isaiah 40:31

CHAPTER 8

THE WAITING PROCESS

Launching out and taking risk are usually challenging steps. It gives you the opportunity "to do better." As Thomas Edison said, "There is far more opportunity than there is ability." We tend to want to give up in the face of failure or feel sorry for ourselves and plead for pity. We need to know that God wants to do something spectacular in our lives. He is our hope, our way maker, and the answer to our prayers.

I was challenged with a situation that was beyond what I expected. I felt helpless, stressed, and distraught. I had lost my job due to a misunderstanding, in a workplace where I had evidence to show my legitimate business interest. The setting up of this business was not entirely easy, but I managed to do so successfully.

The business was set up with a community focus, and a search was launched, with great feedback and general interest in the service it provided. The process was tiring. However, after much commitment and hard work, the business was doing well. As the business became more successful, I started experiencing a change of attitude within the management. This included the way the business was being managed and controlled on a day-to-day basis.

As time went on, the working conditions became unbearable. Everything became an issue as the popularity of the business increased. There was a lack of professionalism within the business because of gossip concerning my expertise and managerial skills.

I was challenged on every side, and months later I was instructed to leave my position—without any legitimate reasons.

Even though I'd played a very important role in setting up and managing the business to that point, I was not given any opportunity to benefit from the success it was now achieving.

It had been my understanding from the beginning that there were to be some fringe benefits for me, but these promises seemed to have been actually made to mislead me.

When I questioned the issue surrounding my dismissal, I was informed that I had no right to claim anything from the business.

At that moment I felt it was unfair to me. I thought of the time, resources, and money invested, as well as my expertise that had been used in growing the business. The kind of deception that I experienced would surely cause stress and distrust in anyone's life.

> The LORD will give them over to you, that
> you may do to them according to every
> commandment which I have commanded
> you. Be strong and of good courage, do not
> fear nor be afraid of them; for the LORD
> your God, He is the One who goes with you.
> He will not leave you nor forsake you.
> —Deuteronomy 31:5–6

I was livid during the process of the whole scenario and thinking ahead of myself, wondering whether or not I would survive.

Then I decided to hold onto the word of God and depend on Him totally. Friends tried to encourage and support the best way they could, but there was something missing. I was hurting, in pain, stressed, and depressed. Even though the word was in me and I was trying to believe, there was still doubt and fear plaguing my mind.

Remember this when you give over your situation to God: don't try to help God. He doesn't need human help. His promises are faithful, and His ways are not our ways; neither are His thoughts our thoughts. It is what God has said: now we *must* believe it. No matter how difficult our condition is, God *can*. People might say to us that there is no hope, or this is the end of the journey, or we have exceeded our chances. Just say to them, "God can."

Encourage yourself in the Lord, and do good. There are times you will not get it right, but remember that, whatever you go through in this life, there is a learning process, and this process takes time and great effort. It is never tranquil.

The process is like the metamorphosis cycle. In order for the caterpillar to become a beautiful butterfly, it has to go through the process: the hibernating, the toiling, some pain and hardship— but the end result is beautiful.

God's promise is faithful; believe what it says and act on it. Don't be distracted. Be focused, be vigilant, and be accountable to someone you can trust. God himself declares this:

> So shall My word be that goes
> forth from My mouth;
> It shall not return to Me void,
> But it shall accomplish what I please,
> And it shall prosper in the
> thing for which I sent it.
> —Isaiah 55:11

God said, "Let there be light," and light appeared. God created the world and mankind in six days by His spoken word, and on the seventh day he rested. If God can rest, then that goes to show us that we also can rest; we can rest in Him. Through all that is happening in our lives, we need to take time out to rest and recuperate from the hardships of life, the pain and stresses of this world.

What has God promised you today? Do you believe that His promises are "sure and amen" in your life? If so, let God be the center in directing and processing your walk with him. It is not easy to wait on something that has been promised to you. If you trust completely in God and His word, He will honor His promises. He's not a man, that He should lie, and neither the son of man, that He should repent.

Have you received any prophesy (in or outside of a church setting) about what God is going to do in your life, and are you still waiting to see it come through? Remember that God's word will not return unto Him void but will accomplish what it sets out to do. His words must be confirmed to you before and then come back to you as a reminder, to encourage and develop you in your walk with Him.

There are many people who have been warned about God's judgment over their lives and are still walking in disobedience. Again, there are people who God said that He would deliver who are waiting for their breakthrough.

Be encouraged. God's words are final, for He will do what He said He will do. No matter how long the process takes, remember the process of the caterpillar. It took a long time in the cocoon to be processed. There might be some squashing, beating, purging, burning, and bruising, but when the process has ended the final result will be worth it.

It is important to know that preparation is key before the process. Whenever we take on a task or battle, it's essential that we prepare for it: spiritually, emotionally, mentally, and physically. The caterpillar had to prepare itself. It went through a stage of eating the right amount of food to sustain itself before it was ready for the next process.

We need the sustenance of the word of God to prepare us for

that journey, and we need to have our hearts and minds fixed on God and His word to follow through the paths of life.

The word of God is what will sustain us in moving forward. We cannot rely on our own strength; we will fail. His guidance is key, and having the right people with us to encourage and stand with us, we can get through it.

Looking back at the story of Ruth, we see that she was adamant about her decision and determined to be a follower of Naomi.

But Ruth said:

"Entreat me not to leave you,
Or to turn back from following after you;
For wherever you go, I will go;
And wherever you lodge, I will lodge;
Your people shall be my people,
And your God, my God.
Where you die, I will die,
And there will I be buried.
The LORD do so to me, and more also,
If anything but death parts you and me."
—Ruth 1:16–17

Not often do you find people you can make such a commitment to follow, especially if you've been disappointed by someone in the past.

There are people who will associate with you thinking that they are divinely connected to effect change. "Be careful for nothing," and be wise in every decision you make, whether it's a relationship or business one.

Ruth followed Naomi because she saw goodness in her, something that could change her life forever. She saw a future for herself; even though her husband had died, there was something more to receive.

God will open our spiritual and natural eyes for us to see what He wants. He will cause certain people to come into our lives to ignite gifts and callings.

Ruth did not know that she would meet her Boaz through Naomi. However, she perceived something in her spirit, and therefore she said, "Urge me not to leave you!"

We all need to first find that connection with the spirit of God. Pray and ask God to reveal the instructions for moving forward. Pray and ask for the spirit of discernment, the spirit of wisdom and understanding to know the direction of God—where He wants to take you and use you. He is waiting for you. "Urge me not."

I strongly believe that God has given me the ability to dream and most of the time have what I've seen in the dream come to pass. I've written down most of the dreams that have been very significant in my life; these have saved me from making the wrong decisions. I have also had dreams that warned me beforehand what would take place regarding my life, the church, and my family. It's sometimes overwhelming when God engages me in what He is doing and showing me.

The key to success in all that happens is obedience. God doesn't always want us to make sacrifices. I'm not saying that sacrifices are not important, but they should be offered with a heart that is truly repentant and full of love for God. A sacrifice should not be just a hollow ritual. God desires total obedience.

The story of Saul highlights this effect:

> So Samuel said: "Has the LORD as great
> delight in burnt offerings and sacrifices,
> As in obeying the voice of the LORD?
> Behold, to obey is better than sacrifice,
> And to heed than the fat of rams.
> —1 Samuel 15:22

In 2006 I had a dream about a man forcing himself into my room. I was taken aback by the decision I made in my dream. I was standing at the door of my room while the man was actually pushing and forcing himself in. When he eventually got in, I raised an alarm and shouted, "I am a woman of God! You cannot stay in my room." He forced himself right in and jumped onto my bed. I quickly rushed out and said, "I will not stay in this house with you." At that time I saw the face and image of the man and what he was all about. I wrote the dream down and left it, not thinking it was anything serious.

In 2009, three years later, I was introduced to a gentleman by chance. We spoke on the phone; he was very keen on meeting, and so was I. We started to get to know each other, and things were looking great. He met with my spiritual covering and told him that he was interested in me. He spoke to my dad on the phone, and my dad asked to meet with him. This was a good start for both of us.

A few months later we were engaged. *Wow! I'm going to get married!* I thought. I was excited, as I had waited faithfully. I was finally to be married—or that's what I thought. Then God stepped in. He had another plan for me. I was busy preparing for the wedding: shopping for dresses, looking at venues, and attending to the never-ending list of wedding-related errands. Everyone was excited for me, but among all of that excitement, something didn't seem right. In the midst of the planning, counselling, and getting to know each other better, I could not figure out what was wrong.

I was more mature in the faith than he was. Some issues came up, which we were trying to deal with in a godly way. His attitude and behavior started to appear strange. I still wasn't sure about what was taking place. Although we prayed together, we attended counselling together, and we were getting to know each other better, something was not settled in my spirit. Then I started seeking the face of God for an answer. I delayed the planning process and the long hours of communication on the phone, and I started to commune more with God and inquire for answers.

You see, it's a very easy decision to continue the process toward getting married when you have been single for so long and the pressures of life surround you. Also, when people wish for you to get married and it seems as if it's finally happening, all your focus is on walking down that aisle with someone by your side, because that big day has finally arrived.

It could happen to anyone, but the truth is that you have a connection with God. It cannot just happen the way you or other individuals want it to. I realize that my life is not my own. I belong to a greater source, and His name is Jesus Christ. I cannot afford to lose out on what we have, since I fell in love with the King.

Thus my prayers went like this: "Lord, if this man is truly my husband, let your will be done." From the very beginning of our relationship, I had been praying this prayer. Then the Lord took me back to the dream I'd had in 2006, and I was completely baffled. Lord, what are you really saying to me now? Suddenly everything unfolded right before my eyes. The person I'd seen in my dream was the same man I was engaged to get married to—*wow, Lord, wow!*

While all this was going on, I went away for a weekend at a ladies' spa retreat that I attended every year. The night before I got there, I stayed at a friend's house. I shared some of what I had been experiencing and my current feelings about the situation. We both got emotional as she began to share a dream she'd had about me. She was very worried about the step I was about to take with this marriage. She was desperate to have fellowship with me so she could share her dream. In the meantime, out of her concern for my life, she was very angry about the decision I had taken to get married to this man. But I had already received the answer from God, and the decision was now up to me to make.

We prayed and cried out to God that night, and I was totally broken. I went to the retreat and came back still broken because of the decision I had to make. When you have to make the right decision in life, it is never easy. It may seem easier to remain in the situation.

The Bible tells us of a story of four men with leprosy who were outcast and didn't have anyone or any place to live. Their situation was devastating, and they had come to a point where they had to make a decision to do or to die. Some people will choose to die in such a situation while others may choose to escape for their lives. The lepers decided to take a step of faith and to receive what God had planned for them.

They did not know what lay ahead of them, so they took that faith walk and went to see what was out there, even though danger was inevitable. But God was just waiting for them to make that faith step so He could deliver them out of their circumstances.

> Now there were four leprous men at the entrance
> of the gate; and they said to one another, "Why
> are we sitting here until we die? If we say, 'We
> will enter the city,' the famine is in the city, and
> we shall die there. And if we sit here, we die also.
> Now therefore, come, let us surrender to the
> army of the Syrians. If they keep us alive, we
> shall live; and if they kill us, we shall only die."
> —2 Kings 7:3–4

They decided to do something and move forward, because their current situation was uncomfortable for them, and it only took one step of faith.

Mine was the hardest resolution for me to choose and adhere to. I remember clearly sitting next to my fiancé in the car and how nervous I felt as I was about to tell him what the Lord had revealed to me. Just imagine how the lepers felt when they were about to visit the camp of the Arameans.

I must admit that I didn't want to proceed with it, but I had to be obedient to God. I told my fiancé what God had revealed to me, not in the full details but enough for him to understand. In conclusion I said, "Let us both go away and seek God, to know what He wants us to do further. But for now He wants us to postpone the wedding until further direction from Him."

This wasn't easily taken by him. He became really angry, and I could understand his pain, because I was torn in between. Days passed that seemed like torture, and I was wondering to myself whether I had made the right decision—it was shattering! I could not measure the pain I felt at that time, and I felt as if I were carrying his pain as well. I was unable to comprehend why the Lord had allowed me to go through the process. Why hadn't He stopped me from getting engaged in the first place?

Since I wasn't sure who this man was, I had many unanswered questions. Somehow, things started to change, and I saw a different person, with strange attitude. God then showed me what He had allowed me to escape because of my obedience.

You may be in a situation or relationship and think that it's too late—there is no way out, and the easier option is to remain where you are, because there is no hope. The enemy (Satan) will deceive you. The Bible clearly states that the enemy is like a roaring lion seeking whom he may devour. Don't get caught up in the enemy's trap. Be watchful, be vigilant, be alert, and most of all, be obedient.

> Be sober, be vigilant; because your adversary
> the devil walks about like a roaring
> lion, seeking whom he may devour.
> —1 Peter 5:8

The scripture clearly says "your enemy the devil"—not your family and not your brothers and sisters in Christ or anyone else. Satan will deceive you and cause you to think that individuals are against you and that God doesn't see and understand what you are going through. Remember this: "The devil is a liar."

There is nothing too hard for God; you are not alone. God wants you to be at a point in your life when you are totally in His will, walking with Him and totally trusting and depending on Him, not others.

There are people who will disappoint you and let you down, but not in all cases. You could have genuine people who stand with you and back you up and pray with you; they stand with you and war against the enemy with you. There may also be those who weep with you when you have troubled times. As the statement goes in Ruth's story, "Urge me not to go."

Break yourself away from your past hurts and pain, and let them be stepping stones to your success in the future. Your *mess* will become a *message* for someone.

You might be thinking that it is too late now: You've already refused to obey, you've gone through it, you've refused to follow God's instruction, and there is no way forward. *No!* God has another plan for you: He wants to turn it around for you. He wants to shift your mourning into dancing and your sorrow into joy.

You have turned for me my
mourning into dancing;
You have put off my sackcloth and
clothed me with gladness,
To the end that my glory may sing
praise to You and not be silent.
O Lord my God, I will give
thanks to You forever.
—Psalm 30:11–12

The decision is to be made by you: what do you want God to do for you? He knows all about it: "'For I know the plans I have for you,' declares the Lord" (Jeremiah 29:11 NIV).

There is a way to escape through every trap of the enemy, a way to recovery. You can recover from the worst situations that you have encountered within your marriage, workplace, home, family, or personal affairs of your life.

Have you ever felt stifled in your life when certain things or decisions you made caused you to stop thinking that God cared or heard you when you called upon him in time of need?

The truth is that His word still stands, no matter how we feel or how things seem to be. The race is not for the swift—it's not about how much we have acquired or the positions we are in. God is still God. God doesn't see us for what we have received in this life, because all that is temporal. He sees and knows what is eternal, because He is God.

The omnipotent, the omniscient, the all-seeing, all-knowing God—He is our sovereign God. He favors us and brings us to a place where all we can do is give Him thanks and praise for what He has done. What seems impossible to man, He has made possible—for all things to work together for the good of those who love Him and are called to His divine purpose.

CHAPTER 9

TIMING MATTERS

One of my favorite bible stories is in the book of 1 Samuel 1; it's the story of Hannah's life. Her name carries a significant meaning, which is *grace*. She was a woman of integrity, honesty, truth, loyalty, faithfulness, commitment, love, strength ... and the list goes on. This woman has taught me a great deal about life, and I was able to take on board some of her attributes, in fact, all through my Christian journey.

Hannah was fervent in worship, very effective in prayer, and willing to follow through even on a costly commitment—even though she struggled with her sense of self-worth because she was unable to have children.

Like many women today who struggle because they are unable to have children, she was ridiculed and teased by individuals around her. Situations like this can make life even more difficult for these women. Even though Hannah was frustrated and annoyed by her competitor, Peninnah, who was able to bear children for their husband, Elkanah, she was determined to trust God to deliver her from her situation.

In those days, polygamy was the norm; it was in existence amongst God's people, even though it often caused serious family issues, as we see in the story of Hannah. There was a purpose in her pain, a reason for her struggles, because the child who would be born from her womb would become a true man of God. This child would grow up to assist Israel's transition from a loosely governed tribal people to a monarchy.

God had kept Hannah's womb closed for a season, because it was a part of His plan. He postponed her years of childbearing to move ahead with a greater plan. It's about God's timing for your life, not yours. God's timing is perfect; He knows when, and He knows how. There is a time for everything.

As a Jamaican, I grew up knowing a little about planting and reaping in the right season. I'm aware that in agriculture there is a season for planting, another for waiting, and a time for reaping. You cannot expect a seed to produce its crop outside its time and season.

When groundwork is completed, the stature of the construction is already determined. It is imperative that we lay proper and solid foundations that can carry the weight of the blessings to come. Very often we are not ready for the blessings God has for us, so when they come we do not see them, and they pass over those of us who are blindfolded.

I've said it before that His plans are good. He knows the end from the beginning. Do not disturb your own future by launching out when you should be going through your waiting and introductory season. When you are flying in an aircraft, you will notice that before the takeoff the engine must reach its full speed, or else it will crash. In general, we are not patient. We want to quickly clutch onto what we perceive in our spirits and run, without direction, from the Lord. We must "in the flesh" wait for the proper season. "But those who wait on the Lord shall renew their strength" (Isaiah 40:31).

There are three simple necessities regarding waiting on God. Such waiting shall cause you to

1. Walk without fainting
2. Run and not be weary
3. Soar (fly) like the eagle

Many people have fainted physically. It is usually caused by a disturbance in blood circulation due to fatigue, pain, shock, or blood pressure. In the spiritual realm, many faint and do not realize that it keeps them from reaping, now and in eternity, what God desires. We are promised to reap in "due season" if we faint not (Galatians 6:9). There are so many things in this life that we must not allow to cause us to pass out or faint, spiritually speaking.

We are prone to stumbling, especially at a time when we are running toward God's plans for our lives. We are weak during the process because of the challenges we see. Though we are God's people, in our spiritual lives we are at times weak. We face the enemies of the world. We face the enemy of our own sinful flesh and lustful desires. And how many times do we fall before these enemies?

We stumble. We don't fall completely, because God's hand is always there to catch us. We do not fall so far down as to perish in hell. But we do stumble. We are tempted to walk out of the way, the straight and narrow path of righteousness that God has set before us.

We need to be like the eagle and have the fearless spirit of a conqueror! We need to see ourselves as overcomers, not people who *are* overcome by the trials of life. We don't need to live in fear of what we see below.

We're all going to face adversity in our lives, and it's the hard times we go through that eventually make us "eagle Christians who soar." That is because we grow through adversity; and God wants us to grow and be all that we can be. It's His will for each of us to reach our full potential in life.

You must begin to wait in expectation—which the vision is yet for an appointed time. You know that *God's timing is always the best.*

It's imperative that you wait, like a waiter in a restaurant, providing service to God and mankind. God obviously has a plan for your life, and if you listen to Him and allow His Spirit to work in you and through you, then you will experience His purpose for your life. "For I know the plans I have for you," declares the LORD, "plans to prosper you and not to harm you, plans to give you hope and a future" (Jeremiah 29:11 NIV).

There is a time for everything, and a season for every activity under heaven.

> To everything there is a season,
> A time for every purpose under
> heaven: A time to be born,
> And a time to die;
> A time to plant,
> And a time to pluck what is planted.
> —Ecclesiastes 3:1–2

God knows what's really best for us; He will not give us more than what we can carry. There are people who are struggling in their situations, thinking God is not there and has deserted them. To these people I say, "You stop there for a few minutes! God hasn't given up on you. Remember that timing is everything, and what you are going through is not for you; it's for the development of those around you. It might be a community, it might be a family, or it might even be a country or an individual. In the process of it all, wait for God's release and timing; then you will see the end results."

Think about those individuals in your country, community, workplace, and family who are stressed with God's timing in answering their prayers. They need your love and support. If you start to support those who are struggling, you may be able to help them remain steadfast in their faith and develop confidence in God's scheduling to bring fulfilment to their lives.

When Jesus told His disciples it was time to cross over the Sea of Galilee, He did not tell them of the storm ahead; neither did it influence His understanding of where He was going. Moreover, in Habakkuk 3:17–19 we are encouraged, that in spite of the frustrations, disappointments, and disillusionments in life, we should "rejoice in the Lord" because He will cause us "to walk upon high places" and run upon the sea without fear and doubt.

It does not matter how hard the experience is or how long we have been in our present location, situation, and circumstances; we can still move on. We can stand and pursue the purpose that God has planted in our way. Most of the time we stay too long in our comfort zones and do not cross over due to the perceived dangers along the way. But thereby we lose the potential benefits at the other side, which were rightfully developed for us to partake of.

It's about God's fulfilment and purpose for you and others. It's not what you can receive for yourself as a person but what God can do through you and for you in the midst of the situation. It's not that Hannah's husband didn't love her; in fact, he loved her more than his other wife. He loved her dearly and was worried for her but could do nothing to help her situation. In spite of that, Hannah trusted God, whom she believed in. She knew that He would come through for her no matter what the issues were and how difficult it seemed to the natural eyes of man. God has the final say.

There will be times in your life when you are judged by others based on what they see from the outside or assume by their feelings toward you. It happens very frequently, even within the church setting. But we need to know who we are, and we need to make up our minds to continue the race, knowing that there is a great reward in the long run. There is always a light at the end of the tunnel.

At times I have been judged by the way I look. I can be very serious, and my countenance will appear to others to be unapproachable, but when they approach me and get to know me, they see a different person. There are times I'd be thinking and my facial expression would change because of the thoughts I was having at the time. I'd try to explain, but some people would not understand my explanation.

It's important to understand each person's individual temperament; when you do it changes the way you think and approach them. God created everyone to be unique, and it is vital that you seek to know the individuals and accept them for who they are, not to change them for your benefit.

We need to be mindful of the things we hold in our hearts and minds toward people. We must seek God and ask him for the spirit of discernment, so we can see and know before we approach.

I, too, had the problem of judging people by what I saw through my natural eyes and then getting involved when I shouldn't. It was none of my business to encounter or interfere in their affairs without the direction of the Holy Spirit. I had to seek the face of God and cry out to him for help. I had to change my attitude and my ways of doing things without His direction and leading.

It was difficult to acknowledge that there was a problem and learn to take it to the Lord in prayer. When I started seeking God to deliver me from that, He began to make changes in my life; it was a process of change for me.

After I embraced changes in my life, others around me were able to see the difference, and they began to accept them. Hannah was also judged and criticized for her countenance, but she continued to trust her God. She did not need to change for man's satisfaction; all she needed to do was pursue her belief in the word of God.

Hannah's conversation with God was even criticized by the priest who judged her incorrectly. In many cases, this is what people do to us. But our situations don't determine our futures.

If we could look at the story in depth, we would see the determination of a person who had been hard hit by the way of life of everyone around her. This woman exercised patience in a tremendous way. She was barren, while her husband had another wife who bore him children and teased her about it.

We are not superhuman, and certainly Hannah wasn't. We can be pushed into things that will cause us to retaliate. However, it wasn't the same for this unique individual, as she had an intimate relationship with her maker. She believed that one day change would come and that the test that she was currently experiencing was just temporary. I strongly believe that nothing lasts forever—only a good salvation and solid relationship with God.

When we don't know what lies ahead for us, the enemy will bring distraction into our paths. He will try to manipulate the changes about to take place in our lives when we display the right attitude during transition.

We need to have the mind of Christ in order to get through the changes we are going to encounter. Understanding changes can be difficult, but when you do, you will be able to maintain the right attitude during transition.

The process is like a chick in its shell trying to break out. When it has made its first crack, it has to continue the process by kicking its way through to success. If the chick gives up, it will eventually die. All hope will be lost because of lack of strength and motivation.

There will be times when God allows us to be on our own for the reason of increasing our strength in Him. We need to refuse to stay in our shells. We must use every force to push past the crack and not sit and die in the shell that is there to birth us into something new.

Christ knew us long before we knew ourselves. We are all sinners, formed in sin and shaped in iniquity. We were slaves to sin before Christ came, and now we have been made free by the redemption of His blood (Romans 6:17).

The truth about Christ and the benefit He wants for us is indicated in His word that formed the doctrine of truth. God wants the best for us. He has destined for us to enjoy wealth and prosperity, which never come easily but through persecution, challenges, ridicule, misunderstanding, long-suffering, stress, pain, and hurt. But in the end is great success.

As we venture through the process of our journeys, we might call this a "discreet long-suffering." Considering again the story of Hannah, you will notice how she simply endured the unrighteous treatment that was displayed to her by Peninnah, her husband's second wife.

The treatment was so intense that resentment led Hannah to believe her husband was oblivious to the torture. His perception about Hannah's misery and grief was totally misplaced. He believed that Hannah was grieving because of her barrenness and did not know that she had already petitioned God and was in her waiting area, praising God for her change to be manifested.

Note here the importance of total silence before God when you are waiting for an answer. You cannot let your guard down and let everyone come in to judge you while you are grieving in the situation or believing in the answer to come. Hannah did not broadcast her grief to anyone—not even the priest and certainly not her husband. No one knew the measure of her pain, as she just suffered quietly. This state of waiting while you suffer is not recommended for every situation.

God requires our full attention when we are at the place of sorrow and shame. He wants to reach out to us in our darkest moments. He beacons to us, indicating to not focus on the crowd but to concentrate on Him.

According to the scriptures, whilst the children of Israel were on their journey God sent a cloud before them. There was a sea between where they were and where God wanted them to be. There will be seas, so there will be waves and there will be winds. Don't let the storms of life constrain you to stay in your place of misery and say, "Well, I'm not crossing over; we are not going to make it." You need a fresh anointing to cross over the barricades of your life.

There may be a sea that you are struggling through. It may be the sea of an impossible boss. The sea may be a tottering marital life, a physical ailment, a business loss, a recalcitrant child, or failure of examinations. It may also be the sea of a person who lacks understanding of where you are going. Don't let any sea stop you.

The word of God admonishes us: "For a just man falls seven times, and rises up again" (Proverbs 24:16).

Micah 7:8 confirms this: "Rejoice not against me, O mine enemy: when I fall, I shall arise; when I sit in darkness, the Lord shall be a light unto me."

> I will also tear off your veils and deliver My
> people out of your hand, and they shall no
> longer be as prey in your hand. Then you shall
> know that I am the LORD. Because with lies you
> have made the heart of the righteous sad, whom
> I have not made sad; and you have strengthened
> the hands of the wicked, so that he does not
> turn from his wicked way to save his life.
> —Ezekiel 13:21–22

God will protect His people regardless of the situation. It can be very tempting for us to be carried away and forget who is guiding us. We need to know who our true leader is and stop following the crowd. There is a right crowd and a wrong crowd.

The right crowd should be directed by God and will lead to the right path. The wrong crowd will distract you, discourage you, detour you, delay you, and derail you. It is important for you to know who you should follow and give your ear to.

Your strength and motivation can be lost during this process of facing your storm. Therefore you must follow the direction of the Holy Spirit and wait for His guidance. The waiting is always rewarding, but it takes great patience to accomplish a good result, which is already given to us before its time. It's not always easy to understand how God performs His will and purpose for us. We constantly need to seek heaven's understanding for the wondrous plan we are going to walk out. Due to lack of understanding, we often cause delay in the time line as we play catch-up to what heaven has been saying all along.

Glitches in our lives may be good. We should aim to embrace and love the storms in our lives. Many life situations come with troubles and trials; however, they arise in our life cycles to make us stronger and wiser.

Whenever misfortune occurs, the word of God declares that "He will be a present help in times of trouble." *Present help* simply means that He is always there, even before the storm approaches us.

We often don't like to speak of persecutions or moving through the rough edges of being persecuted. But persecution will allow us to mature spiritually, prosper in the things of God, and be empowered in His will.

During my experiences going through the seas in my life, I realized that judging someone based on their reaction to a situation is the wrong approach. It is always good to wait on the Lord's direction before making the move toward others. I recognize now that timing is important for breakthrough.

CHAPTER 10

THE PROCESS IN THE WAITING ROOM

The story of Jesus calming the storm after asking the disciples to come away with Him from the crowd is cited in Mark 4:35–41. This was an unexpected situation for the disciples, because they were not aware of what was impending. However, they still followed Jesus and ventured over to the "other side."

Moving to the other side may force you to change and grow. Some of the disciples were known as experienced fishermen; additionally, they were becoming accustomed to life and whatever experiences went with it. In this situation, Jesus wanted them to have an unfamiliar experience within their comfort zone.

Then a threat of unfamiliarity began without any warning. An uncomfortable feeling struck—a time of stretching, trouble, struggle, and testing. Does that sound familiar to you? When the seas of our lives don't look normal, signs of trouble are presented in the atmosphere that can provoke panic, anxiety, and terror.

The first thing we consider in such a situation is what to do and how to get through it. Our focus starts to become self-centered, not realizing that Christ is on the scene. He is present, He is in the center, He is right in the storm with us—yet we choose to worry rather than calling on the name of Jesus.

Even though the story of the disciples makes reference to a physical storm, we frequently go through personal storms. These occur in many different ways, some of which we are not prepared for.

Presently you might be having various confrontations of stormy situations in your life; here are two options I'd like to introduce to you.

Option 1: You can worry and drag yourself to depression, crying your eyes out while assuming that Jesus no longer cares.

Option 2: You can select the path of resistance to the enemies fear and anxiety and put your trust in Him. Whenever you feel like panicking, you can confess your needs to God and trust Him to care for you. He desires that you call upon Him in severe times of need and struggle.

It might be the case that you have been serving God for many years and have not yet experienced struggles in your life. Suddenly one day something unfamiliar starts to occur in your life that causes you to divert your attention from God and begin to focus on the problem.

This appears to be more difficult than you would have imagined. Do not underestimate God's power to handle crises in your life. Even though the disciples did not experience Christ's power to the fullest, we cannot allow ourselves to lose out the access we have to connect to the higher source.

When we are connected, we can draw enough strength in our spirits to activate the power of God to push through our stormy period. That will enable us to walk on the water without fear and tunnel through our troubled season.

It is time to activate the power of prayer in our lives and target the spiritual winds that are blowing in our surroundings—the winds of poverty, joblessness, and sickness. In their anxiety, the disciples called upon Jesus immediately for help, and He rose up to the call and rebuked the wind and commanded it to be still. Now we need to activate the authority that Christ gave us when he died and rose again. We have the authority to bind and to loose.

> Assuredly, I say to you, whatever you bind on
> earth will be bound in heaven, and whatever
> you loose on earth will be loosed in heaven.
> —Matthew 18:18

With the power of Jesus Christ in us, we can take authority over sickness and disease. We can command a situation to change by the power of the blood of Jesus. It will make a difference when we decide to speak the undiluted word of God into our existence. It is not wise for anyone to remain in a storm.

Therefore, reject the complacent, disheartening lifestyle in which you become trapped without any sign of forward motion. Right where you are now, take that step of faith, and begin to walk on the water of freedom.

Escape the deception of the boat and the box mentality you have entrapped yourself in. Believe in your heart that it is time to get out of the box. Move forward into something greater and bigger, more than you have experienced before.

God is relocating you to the land of greatness, where you will experience abundance. There will be no more begging or desiring to eat from the leftovers or crumbs that have fallen from the table.

It is now time to sit comfortably around the table of success and favor that God has prepared for you. Psalm 23 emphasizes that God is a caring shepherd and a dependable guide. You are required to follow Him and obey His commands. He is your only hope for eternal life and security.

A dear friend of mine shared her story with me some time ago. She commented on having had her own fair portion of challenges, hurts, abuse, and betrayals. She started by giving a few pointers to say that if you have your health, mental willpower, and faith in Christ Jesus, you have everything.

She described how, as time went by, she learned to accept the way things were going in her life and the way people behaved in her surroundings. She said we need to understand that not everything is going to be the way we want it to be. If we cannot accept reality, we will feel very frustrated with life. Many people will try to change someone or something that they cannot control, and when it doesn't work out, they resolve toward being unhappy.

We seem to always need to be part of a change or transition. Change is necessary; we are often tempted to celebrate the victory of the past when we begin to embrace future endeavors. We could sit down with the past victory and miss the triumph of the hour, or we could embrace the new beginnings of life. God is not busy worrying about how we will pay our rent. He supplies the means for everything we require. All we need is to know how to get it—by believing and trusting him.

The minute we accept reality we become competent to confront our challenges. That allows us to think further and more clearly about how to advance toward our goals every day. Referring to my friend's situation, my advice on it is to avoid believing that you can accept everything that crosses your pathway.

Don't agree to that notion to move forward. Do not feel comfortable with what the enemy throws at you—take a stand and fight. The disciples of the boat did not accept the storm. They called for backup; they approached the source their help came from. It's important that you know what to accept and what to reject in life.

Further on in her statement, my friend mentioned giving her life a different meaning by learning to accept diverse alterations all the time. Many people don't like diversion, which leads to change; they resist because it redirects them outside of their comfort area. They may be unhappy or happy in life at a certain stage; however, they should realize that the situation is not permanent.

You must aim to train your mind to be at peace continuously, regardless of the emotional state you are experiencing. Overcoming traumas and hurts is a healing process; you need to take your time and allow yourself to feel and accept those emotions. Then learn to deal with the situation and let it go. These are her own words: "I didn't give up. I kept on fighting and believing that things would change. I refused to be a victim, and therefore I started to reach out to people who motivated me, i.e., my mother, family, life coaches, friends, and church members who were inspiring."

This lady has been a close friend for some time now, and I can testify to her strength, both physically and spiritually. She learned to trust in God during the most difficult storms in her life. I didn't mention her situation in detail for confidentiality purposes, but the lesson she learned was to trust in God.

No matter how difficult our struggles are, God knows, and He cares. For many years I held onto this quote: "You must go through it in order to tell it." Do not stop pushing because you feel defeated. Remember this: we are duty-bound to continue pushing forward until we receive our breakthrough. It's time to center our minds on what is ahead, even though it may not be clearly in sight; but we should wait for the green light to victory.

In Isaiah 54:1 it speaks of the song of a barren woman, a cry from the unfruitful expressed in a song to God. Since the situation existed, this means life didn't stop there. Rise up and sing, shout and rejoice in your pain. It may sound crazy, but it works.

This chapter speaks of various messages, but the one that really stands out for me concerns birthing forth in your barren season. This is not the end; it's the beginning of greatness, success, and prosperity. Barren means unproductive, infertile, unfruitful, and desolate. It is usually a state of a woman having no children, an inability to conceive and a man's inability to impregnate.

Birthing forth (or bringing forth) has to come through conception. Barrenness can be spiritual as well as physical. If you are barren and unable to conceive (spiritually), you need divine intervention through the blood of Jesus. We often confuse ourselves with spiritual versus natural possessions.

The Bible clearly states, "For we wrestle not against flesh and blood but against principalities, against powers, against the rulers of the darkness of this age, against spiritual hosts of wickedness in the heavenly places" (Ephesians 6:12).

I was given the opportunity to minister at a women's retreat in London on the topic of birthing through conception. We were about twenty in a conference room at a hotel where we stayed for the weekend. That day after I spoke, women were left wailing as they gave birth to their spiritual babies. I taught how important it is to protect whatever you are carrying and that there can be times when the conception process is hard to get to.

Life can be so difficult for some people; it will leave them in a state of barrenness even though they are desperate to give birth. Church situations and conditions of family life can lead people to a place of abandonment.

I expressed myself openly to these women, without shame, and I shared the harshness of my barrenness at that time in my life. I remember at one point in my life being unable to look in the mirror and feel comfortable about myself. I talked about the time when I just accepted whatever people were saying about me and did not believe the truth of God's word in my life.

Some of the women could connect to my experience. The room was very quiet as they listened attentively to the message I brought to them. I then asked everyone to find themselves a birthing partner, and they positioned themselves as supporting midwives to the women in "labor." At first they didn't take it seriously, and then something strange began to happen in the atmosphere.

Some of the women began to wail as a sign of giving birth. Some were in pain because they had been left barren and had not reached a place of conception.

The fires of God ignited the room, and His power began to manifest. It went for a while, and some women were left broken and needed to be ministered to. Whether it was physical barrenness or spiritual, God showed up that day, and even when the next speaker came on, we still felt the presence of God through His power of delivery.

Barrenness can relate to different areas in our lives. We can be led into open shame based on the positions we find ourselves in. These could be situations in which we are blocked from keeping a job, having good health, keeping a relationship, or sustaining a marriage, or they could be other downfalls that occur in our world. We might be facing any one of these situations, and if so, there is help for us.

God, our Savior, is compassionate; He is the God of second chance in any area you may be stuck in. He told us He would supply all our needs according to His riches in glory. God is not short in supply; He has everything in abundance, to the point of overflow. Nothing is too difficult for Him to do for you. If you mention the word and place a demand on it, you will receive your reward if you stay in the queue toward victory.

In the story of Sarah, it wasn't the right time for her. As the story unfolds in Genesis 15, we learn how God had a plan to give Sarah and Abraham a child, according to His promise. Sarah took matters into her own hands and chose to fill the void in her life by promoting her maiden to her husband to give them a child. In other words, she allowed another woman to take her place, not a woman of her rank but her maid.

We can be so desperate for what we want in life that we end up choosing incorrectly and losing sight of the consequences of our decisions. We must be careful what we wish for and what we do to receive it. The result can be costly and dangerous, not just to ourselves but to all those who are attached to our destiny.

If we view the spiritual aspect of the waiting and planning process of our Christian walk, we may realize that we are choosing to do things our way without the direction of God. When the Bible tells us to seek first the kingdom of God and all His righteousness and then instructs us that all things shall be added, it clearly means we should ask and wait. Since we are unable to produce what we desire while we are on our journeys (or to wait in the process) our desire leads us to the shortest routes. We may end up jammed in potholes where we are incapable of moving ahead, which forces us to commence the journey all over again.

My friend, the conditions of life are never easy. Waiting on God is never easy, struggling in a bad marriage is never easy, being jobless is never easy, losing a family member or a best friend is never easy, and living in an abusive relationship is certainly not easy to handle—*but* God can make a difference!

God has equipped every one of us with the ammunition to push ourselves and bring forth what has already been placed inside of us. Hence it is time to conceive; the conception process must begin first. You have a dream, you have a plan, and you have the ideas. Is it a great vision of something inside of you? Right now, God is saying to us that whatsoever He has conceived in us, it's time to give birth!

Don't accept the fact that you are barren. Say no to barrenness and yes to fruitfulness. Arise to the challenge of your destiny; the time to smile again is now. It's time to sing again, oh barren woman. God has permitted you to have many children (breakthroughs). He has changed your destiny and turned your mourning into dancing again and all your sorrow into exceedingly great joy. Rejoice, somebody, and give Him praise—*Hallelujah!*

God does not accomplish His purpose and plans only by measurements and then just leave you halfway. Whatever He has commenced in you, He will always complete it. He's not a man that He should lie; when He says yes or no, nobody can change it; His word is final. Our Father knows us all; before we were conceived in our mothers' womb He had a destiny for each of us.

Now we are carrying a child (destiny), that gift, the anointing, the ministry; it is time to give birth.

During this process it is important to take note of what to do next. You must diet on healthy food, the spiritual nourishment that comes from the word of God; you must surround yourself with wise experience, believers, and those who see greatness in you and desire to see you delivered safely into your destiny. Your vessel is delicate; therefore, whatever you are carrying is precious. Do not allow the enemy to interfere with the process. Giving birth is a very painful yet rewarding sensation.

Although I'm not a mother and wasn't fortunate enough to give birth to a child in the natural, I personally can testify that my journey so far has allowed me to give birth to many spiritual children. With no regrets, I celebrate the goodness of our God, who has triumphantly succeeded in granting me this experience on my journey with Him.

The experience I had strengthened me to wait for many years, even in the toughest and most painful moments. I was able to push my way through the rough edges. Circumstances allowed me to surround myself with great spiritual midwives who could help me bring forth my gifting and my fulfilled destiny during the crucial part of my birthing process.

Whenever you are told to push, prepare for some serious pain and suffering. You cannot afford to stop during the process; otherwise you will terminate the greatest joy and reward you've been waiting for. Hence, you must push in an extensive manner, in anticipation of your delivery. One of the important procedures in labor is the travailing method, which is the language spoken when prayer is involved. It is a guaranteed manifestation when you pray your way through a trying period to aim for an innovation in a situation. That means you must P-U-S-H—Pray Until Something Happens!

Before she was in labor, she gave birth;
Before her pain came,
She delivered a male child.
Who has heard such a thing?
Who has seen such things?
Shall the earth be made to give birth in one day?
Or shall a nation be born at once?
For as soon as Zion was in labor,
She gave birth to her children.
—Isaiah 66:7–8

These two verses clearly cement the previous paragraphs. God will not and cannot leave us. His work for restoring us is ongoing. He who has started a good work is faithful to complete it to the end. God has promised to accomplish what He has started, and the process is as unstoppable as giving birth to a baby.

You will go through the process of pain for a while, which is essential; it's an important step in the labor. Then your joy will proceed in the morning. From time to time it will become difficult to wait for the morning course, but do not feel downhearted; hold on and push harder. It will result in great joy when your morning comes to light.

A message came through the prophet Isaiah, whom God has judged and given the opportunity of hope. The prophesy came to existence in the couple of verses above; it explains the coming victory of those who have been through great ordeals.

Your solution is in progress. At the end, your child will eventually become that promised one who will bring a shock to the world. The world is waiting for your child, the one whom you have given labor to. It will contribute greatly in this season, to heal and deliver and make free those who are bound in captivity.

Yet in all these things we are more than
conquerors through Him who loved us.
—Romans 8:37

Isaiah 66 verse 8 asked, "Who has heard such a thing?" It is a question that will cause you to ponder on what is coming next. It was mentioned that she will give birth but without pain. How can this be? Who has heard of such a thing? Victory and deliverance will happen so quickly that not even pain will have time to stand in the pathway. What we consider to happen in years will take effect in a minute. God is now working on some sudden victories for you, and shame will no longer be your label.

Lack will now take a backseat, and your tears will be of joy, not sorrow. Poverty suddenly will make a U-turn, and then God will manifest Himself in great power and strength for His dearly beloved.

God will not leave incomplete His work of rebuilding His people. In this image of birth, God shows that He will achieve what he has proposed for you. It is as unrelenting as the birth of a baby; when all the pain is over, then the joy commences.

The time of your deliverance, victory, and vindication has truly come to the surface. It is very important to guard your victory when you receive it. Be aware of the spiritual wolves that disguise themselves in sheep clothing; they are sent out to destroy what you have birthed in the ministry of your life. The gift or ministry you have birthed and carried will be an attraction to the nation; therefore, beware of the demolishers of dreams and vision, the ones who will envy you and be jealous of what God has given you.

God will set you in a position from which you can receive an instant blessing, and that reward will attract many other believers and unbelievers. Anything you have accomplished through God will be so powerful that you can cause damage to the enemy and his kingdom if you use the power correctly.

CHAPTER 11

SPIRITUAL VIRUSES

Sometimes as we work really hard within our ministries, we can unexpectedly get caught in a trap that the enemy has set. This happens because of blind-sightedness, which we all should be mindful of after giving birth. This is what I call "spiritual viruses;" they can be very contagious in the Christian faith.

In fact, in the natural world there are actually trillions of viruses in our bodies, but they're not all bad.

Scientists have discovered that a virus is a microorganism that can only reproduce within a living organism. Frequently viruses cause infection, but some viruses are good. These are called antiviruses, and they destroy the viruses that are contagious. Many members of the body and spiritual leaders become infected easily by the virus of pride.

I list pride as a virus, because it is so easily transmittable that it can cause spiritual damage. But we need the antivirus of the Holy Spirit to counteract transmission of this contamination. Can you just imagine all the struggles you have been through to get to where you are today? And can you imagine losing more because of pride?

Pride goes before destruction, and
a haughty spirit before a fall.

—Proverbs 16:18

When you are filled with pride, you lean toward your selfish desires and take little account of your weaknesses; you do not anticipate stumbling blocks. The proud often consider themselves to be above the feebleness of common individuals. Ironically, proud people rarely realize that pride is their biggest downfall in life, even though everyone around them is well aware of it.

If you think you might be heading in this direction, ask someone you trust whether self-satisfaction has blinded you to the warning signs. That person may help you escape the stumble that might kill your ministry.

It is very easy to become proud in ministry (or any given gifts which God has entrusted to you). It's a subtle virus, which can cause you to direct great attention to yourself and not God, who has allowed you to be who you are at this point in your walk. Pride must be cast out of your life and placed under subjection through the blood of Jesus Christ.

One of the most dangerous things pride has done to individuals is make them think too highly of themselves and begin to belittle others. In the long term, it will deliver them to open humiliation.

At this moment, just pause and ask God to remove every blemish you have accumulated through pride in your life cycle. Ask him to cleanse you from this virus that was slowly destroying your ministry and give you back the key to surrender your life totally to Him. In this process, you will have a motivational impact in the things of God through compassion and love.

The second spiritual virus that is common among us is hatred. Hatred can be seriously lethal toward others, and it is like a corporate lifestyle within the body of Christ. Our actions at times shout out clearly how much we can despise someone, which leads to hating them.

Hating your brothers and sisters in Christ, or anyone for that matter, does not model the love of God. You can't say to a person, "I do not like you. I just can't be around you; you make me feel sick and uncomfortable." That would clearly display the signs of hate and not love.

> If someone says, "I love God," and hates his brother, he is a liar; for he who does not love his brother whom he has seen, how can he love God whom he has not seen?
>
> —1 John 4:20

From your own mouth it is very easy to say that you love God when that love doesn't cost you anything more than weekly attendance at religious services. However, the real test of your love for God is the way you treat the people right in front of you—that is, family members and believers. You cannot truly love God while you refuse to love those who are created in His image.

Hatred can easily spill over and contaminate the flow of God's love in your life. It will also cause stagnation in your spiritual growth and development as an individual. When God delivers you from certain conditions in your life, you must be aware that the enemy is waiting to lure you right back in, and in most cases it will cause you to be seven times worse than before.

Try not to prejudge someone's actions without knowing the facts, or you will enter a danger zone. The only way out is to show love, because love covers a multitude of sins.

Hating someone will attach itself to lies, which is the third spiritual virus predominant in the Church today. It is clearly speaking about something or someone and making up stories that are not true.

The opposite of truth is a lie. A lie can cause great damage to others who are affected by what comes from your mouth. Proverbs 26:28 says, "A lying tongue hates those it hurts, and a flattering mouth works ruin." When you continue to hate someone, lies begin to spring forth in your heart. This may be unpleasant when you begin to communicate.

Lies can affect your life both physically and spiritually. A lie may seem the easy way out at times, but it's a danger. You may lie to get out of trouble or exaggerate your experience and say things that will make you look good to others, especially if you want to make it in society or feel accepted amongst your peers.

This is how contagious it can be to individuals you are connected to: what you say from your mouth can mean life or death. The Bible says death and life are in the power of the tongue; therefore, if you continue to speak lies, you may kill those around you as well as yourself. Be mindful of what you say, how you say it, and when you say it. Let love be in the center of everything you do in your life.

There are many more spiritual viruses that are very common among us; I've only listed a few. We need Jesus Christ, who is our mediator, to guide us through the rough stages of life and help us stay alive. Thus we protect what we received when we gave birth to our ministry or gift. Whatever it is, do not aim to go back to the same habit and lifestyles you were attached to—the hurts, pains, and struggles. Fight on, because now is the time to work with what God has entrusted to you for protection.

CHAPTER 12

EXPERIENCING THE SPIRITUAL AND THE NATURAL

> But the natural man does not receive the
> things of the Spirit of God, for they are
> foolishness to him; nor can he know them,
> because they are spiritually discerned.
> —1 Corinthians 2:14

This is a testimony that may support you in believing that God works both in the spiritual and the natural. In 2015 I went to the beautiful island of Jamaica, where I had been born. Everything to me was strange and seemed to be out of place.

I had last been there in 2003, when I went back for a short visit while I was living London. This time around, it was on a totally different level for me. My spiritual life had matured in many ways, and I was involved in ministry, filling every gap I could to offer in service of the Lord.

I had already become an ordained minister while in London and so was allowed to bless others in my ministry. I was able to go through this process because of the gifts God had blessed me with. I was anxious and at the same time excited about my journey and the things God had in store for me as I shared with others.

Also around the same period I was asked to preach at an annual convention, which was being held at my former church in Jamaica. I was engaged to a wonderful man of God, who became my husband on August 29, 2015. We got married on the sunny island of Jamaica, which also was my main purpose for being in Jamaica at this time. We had a wonderful wedding day, even though prior to the day many obstacles seemed to block our path. God came through right on time for us, and it was a great success.

The whole process of going to Jamaica to get married and starting a new life was the biggest transition I had ever experienced, and it didn't stop there. It wasn't in the plan to go back to London but to journey to the United States, which would be my new home. I know the story seems far-fetched, but it was because I met my husband-to-be met in London, where I lived, but he resided in the United States.

After we got married and had our honeymoon, it was time for my husband to go back to America to make preparations for me to live there. It took one year before I could join him properly. He made return trips so we could spend time together. Being in Jamaica for one year seemed much longer, since I was trying to readjust myself to the lifestyle of my hometown.

It was very difficult at times, but I trusted God and what His word said to me: "I will never leave you nor forsake you." I remember I cried many nights and asked God to tell me why He had brought me there in that season. But I also continued to thank Him for what He was doing for me.

As mentioned above, I was one of the guest speakers at the church's annual convention. I was excited about that, but at the same time nervousness and fear tried to take over as I viewed the entire group, including a seasoned bishop and other pastors who were scheduled to speak that week. However, I trusted God to deliver me, and He came through for me, as He often did. The word was ministered and souls were blessed that night.

One of my favorite scriptures is found in Jeremiah 29:11

(NIV): "For I know the plans I have for you," declares the Lord, "plans to prosper you and not to harm you, plans to give you hope and a future." Wow! God had a greater plan for me, and I was so self-centered that I could not visualize what was happening around me.

So many things were going through my mind. I had given up my job in London and was serving in the different ministries and not able to see my friends. Even though I was now a married woman, I was still feeling unaccompanied by the things I was so attached to. To my surprise, I thought wrong; at first I forgot who I was and what God had birthed in me, and did not know that He had placed me on an assignment in Jamaica.

In the book of Proverbs (18:16 NIV) it says, "A gift opens the way for the giver and ushers him into the presence of the great." The way was opened for me in Jamaica, and I started giving my service in whatever area was required. I began preaching on many occasions, not only in the church I grew up in but also at other churches on the island. Doors automatically began to open before my eyes, and God started to honor His word in my life. I was seeing hurting men and women who needed answers from God; they were receiving the undiluted word of God.

There were others who needed a friend, a confidant, a shoulder to cry on, and an ear to listen to them—and God was moving mightily. It became overwhelming and emotional for me, but I remained very much aware of the spiritual virus of pride that could attach itself to me. There was a time where it almost did, but God protected me from it.

At this point, the Lord started to show me the conditions of the church. He was revealing to me the broken and sad, the weary and the sick. In the natural world it was all too much for me to handle at the same time; but I stayed connected in the spirit. I remained close to God in order to listen to His voice and adhere to His directions.

I began to minister at crusades, conventions, street meetings, and funerals. My cup was full and running over; I did work with the worship team, and we were transformed in the spirit as God moved in an atomic way, touching lives in the process.

Again I was tempted by the spiritual viruses of pride and lies; this time I was so alert that God gave me the grace to recognize the devices they were coming with. It is so easy to get trapped, and I almost fell prey. However, God reminded me of the assignment He had called me to accomplish. Remembering where God had taken me from in my spiritual life I had to act quickly.

I remembered back in London, where I had been infected by sinful desires of jealousy, pride, and lies. I had been spiritually ill because of these viruses, and even my natural body had become affected; I had been at the point of death spiritually. But thank God for His grace and mercy and those spiritual midwives who nurtured me over the years.

It is very important to attach yourself to those who can speak life into your spirit. Many Christians are dying spiritually because they associate themselves with the wrong people. It is time to ask God to remove the scales from your eyes and allow you to see in the spirit the wolves who disguise themselves in sheep's clothing. Ask for spiritual discernment, and God will surely give it to you.

I met a few individuals who revealed situations that were mind-blowing as they shared their experiences while I ministered to them.

In the churches today there is much spiritual causality; we must be very careful how we handle and treat God's people. A church can at times become a hospital to cater to the needs of the people. Individuals may come in to be healed and delivered, but oftentimes they leave the same way they came—or worse.

The word of God declares, "I will build my church and the gates of hell shall not prevail against it." God will not allow His children to die or be hurt anymore. He has heard the cries of His children and is always ready to rescue them from all struggles as they wait patiently for Him to move in their midst.

Within the process of God moving and everything seeming surreal, I met a couple in Jamaica. (Their names are withheld for the sake of confidentiality.) I asked their permission to share their testimony in my book, and I am honored to do so. This couple had been experiencing barrenness in their lives for some time, both physically and spiritually.

They invited me to their home, as they wanted to share what they were going through. Before I went to their home, God was ministering to me regarding this couple. I really didn't know what they were going through, but each time I saw them, I felt a strong urge to speak to them by the leading of the Holy Spirit.

The day I went to their home, they began to share in-depth the situation they were facing, while I listened closely. Then suddenly the Holy Spirit began to reveal certain things to me, and I started to minister to them individually. One of the issues I will mention here is quite significant; it links to a few chapters back, where we focused on barrenness. This time around the emphasis was on physical barrenness. The couple had been trying to have children, but the woman had been unable to conceive ever since they'd been married a few years past.

What I've learned over the years is that unforgiveness can block you from receiving healing, deliverance, and breakthrough. Unforgiveness can be lethal; you must endeavor to forgive other people—even your worst enemies. If you have a grudge against someone, that is unforgiveness, and if you continue to think evil against someone and refuse to forgive, you are indulging in the area of unforgiveness.

> So Esau hated Jacob because of the blessing with
> which his father blessed him, and Esau said in
> his heart, "The days of mourning for my father
> are at hand; then I will kill my brother Jacob."
> —Genesis 27:41

Esau carried such hatred for his brother that he failed to recognize that it was his own wrongdoing, when he decided to give away his birthright, that had been his undoing. Unforgiveness can be born from our own wrong decisions in life and when we blame others for our mishaps. Because Esau continued to build up hatred, this caused him to make mistakes in his life. In view of this, he missed out greatly on several opportunities that were rightfully his.

When you refuse to forgive someone who has wronged you, it will block your spirit from receiving the freewill to reconcile and move on. I once heard a preacher sharing a story about reconciliation. He said one of the hardest things to do in life is to forgive someone who is not sorry.

This story is about a black woman who had moved into a white community. Her next-door neighbor, who was obviously white, began to throw feces into her yard every day. This happened for months, and the months turned to years. Then one day, the old white woman had a heart attack. The very first person to visit was the black lady from next door, whose yard she had thrown the feces into.

The woman came in carrying a bunch of roses, and the white lady said, "Thank you very much. I don't know whether you know or not that I was the one throwing feces into your yard."

The other woman said, "Yes, I know."

Then the white woman asked, "Did you order these from the local flower shop?"

"No," replied the black woman.

Then she asked her, "Did you order them over the phone?"

Her reply was, "No, these roses are from the feces you threw in my yard. You meant it for evil, but God meant it for good."

It's important to forgive, and when you forgive you will come out smelling like a rose. People will do all kinds of things to you, but remember Jesus: when He died He gave the original forgiveness to those who are being nasty to you.

Now back to the original story about the couple. This woman had unforgiveness in her heart over certain painful issues that she had experienced with those closest to her. After our talk, we were able to understand the importance of forgiveness: if we don't try to reconcile with those who have caused us hurt we will continue to be victims of failure. Even though it was mostly the woman who was affected, I had to ask both of them to forgive all those who had done them wrong and caused them hurt and pain, even if those persons were deceased.

They listed all the names and asked God to forgive all these people. I then began to pray with them. As we reached out to God, we started to renounce every curse that had been placed upon their marriage, things they were aware of and things they were not. We began to bind every curse word that had been spoken over their lives with or without their knowledge.

The spirit of God began to move as we pleaded the blood of Jesus in their home. One of the things I did, while the spirit led, was to open their front door and kick the enemy out of the house. Some people might say, "That is crazy—that's not of God!" or "How can you kick the enemy out when you cannot see him?"

There comes a time in our Christian lives when we need to become radical and take action in some unnatural ways that people may not welcome or understand but God will. I had to take action and prophetically demonstrate the power we have in the name of Jesus. I had to follow the wisdom of God in every given situation. There may be times when you only need to worship God or pray a simple prayer and you will receive the victory.

You see, in the Bible, when Jesus was going around healing and delivering people, things did happen one way only. There were some things Christ did that did not seem right to human eyes, but Christ is the master of everything, and He is in control, not man.

After our prayer, this couple began to feel a peacefulness in their home. I left there with a sense of release for the couple and believing that God had heard our prayers. Approximately two months later, after I had left the island to join my husband in the United States, I received a message on my phone.

The woman informed me that she was pregnant and quite overwhelmed to be receiving her miracle from God. She visited the doctor, went through the pregnancy, and eventually delivered a healthy baby. Not all cases will happen this way, but I guarantee that God will show up to deliver His people.

I don't seek a platform or fame for doing God's work. God can use anyone to perform His work here on earth; He just wants us to make ourselves available to be used at any time and in any season. We give thanks to God for the deliverance and for honoring His word in us. It is important to be obedient to the word of God. It's not just quoting scriptures; it takes living the word of God and being disciplined in serving Him faithfully.

My fellow believer, God is real and He wants the best for us. He wants to take us from nothing and make us become special in Him. How many of you are pregnant today? Are you ready to give birth to your destiny, or are you stuck in a barren situation, where nothing seems to be happening for you? It is time to give yourself a thorough search to diagnose the cause of your misfortunes in life.

There might be blocks in your life, viruses that need attention from our Lord, Jesus Christ. These viruses, as I've mentioned before, can be either infectious or contagious. The infectious virus can be transmitted from person to person, such as by gossiping and slandering each other, which is not healthy for the spiritual man. In some instances the virus can be transmitted by direct contact. Both ways involve an emotional feeling or attitude, which is likely to spread and affect others. We believers must guard and protect ourselves from the things that are treacherous to us.

Let us take a pattern from the behavior of David and Jonathan in the Bible. They protected each other to the very end; Jonathan helped David in the state of his spiritual pregnancy. David was carrying kingship inside of him, and someone had to help him birth his destiny. In the natural there are two things that describe a woman when she is pregnant. She is waiting and expecting. This same process applies to us in the spiritual.

We are *waiting* for our breakthrough and *expecting* victory at the very end. It is easy to get scared in the process of waiting. While you wait in the season of your breakthrough, the developing stages will begin to become obvious. Evidence of development will sometimes cause discomfort and weariness in the various stages.

When God develops us in our ministry, we begin to grow and cultivate skills and patience. We start to improve our lives as we educate ourselves in training for our next step. Training is important for everyone; it allows us to become skilled at what we are giving birth to. If we are good waiters, we will get good tips.

Therefore, we must learn to serve God faithfully while we wait in the developing stage. God has His hands on us; therefore, while we are preparing ourselves for our labor, we should stay away from individuals who will destroy our purpose. Rather, we should stick closely to those who determine to partner with us to the very end.

Your healing is attainable, your freedom is possible, and whatever you need from God is achievable even after a great suffering while pushing forth. The enemy doesn't know your future, only God, your creator—the one who is the master planner for your calling.

Whenever the way forward seems difficult, don't try to force your way into things that are a poor fit for you. If you forcefully push out of situations instead of waiting on God, you will end up in a ditch. If and when God gives you an instruction, you should follow it through.

Each and every time you find yourself at a place where the way ahead is challenging, don't become complacent in that position. If you do, it will become so difficult that one day you will find yourself drifting back in to the state of the ordinary instead of the extraordinary. It may reach to a point at which it becomes harder rather than easier; then you become uncomfortable and, at the same time, familiar.

The book of Galatians tells us that those who were going forward decided to turn back to what was familiar; a familiar lifestyle and habit that seemed very comfortable to revert to.

> But then, indeed, when you did not know
> God, you served those which by nature are not
> gods. But now after you have known God, or
> rather are known by God, how is it that you
> turn again to the weak and beggarly elements,
> to which you desire again to be in bondage?
> —Galatians 4:8–9

These verses clearly asked a couple of obvious questions of the Galatians. To paraphrase, it's saying to them that when they were outside of the will of God they were enslaved by the sinful nature of the world.

Now you are saved and have a relationship with God; you also have tasted of His goodness. Because of what the world throws at you, you may decide to go back to the same standard of living. In Christ you have received the adoption of sons and daughters and the effect of His free and rich grace.

Then why should you choose to go back to the same way of living? Whatever you love and care for the most will become your god, what you choose to worship and live with. This may mean turning back to pleasures and lustful ways, ignorantly resting and trusting in manmade idols and false religions. Thankfully God's mercy is everlasting; He cares for us all, no matter what decisions we make in life.

When things don't happen the way we want, we tend to take

another route. An example of this is when the Israelites wanted to return to Egypt after being liberated from slavery.

Imagine—if God took you out of an abusive relationship or a situation that had trapped you for many years, would you aim to go back because the future was uncertain? You might think that God would not supply your anticipated needs.

God is not a man that He should lie; He is true to His word, and His word is final. God has promised to take care of us. A place awaits us where everything we need is in His will for us. There is a place of freedom and restoration, a place where we can find peace. Why not trust God to work it out for us? Let us not look at those who are not steadfast in His will. Let us look to God, who is the author and the finisher of our faith.

Not everyone is allowed to go where God is taking you. When they find out that you are different, they will pull away from you. When the battle gets intense, they will not fight with you. Most of the time it happens that they battle against you; they will refuse to stand with you when you need them the most. In the long run, you will discover that you are alone and all those who were with you are no more.

This movement will allow you to live by faith and not by what you see; and this explains why going back seems to be the easier option. Know that faith in God and His word will keep you moving forward and bringing you to a place of liberty.

CHAPTER 13

IT'S ATTAINABLE THROUGH FAITH

*For by grace you have been saved, through faith
and that not of yourselves; it is the gift of God.*
—Ephesians 2:8

The heart is the center or innermost part of something. The heart must be pure and right before God. I was asked a very important question by one of my husband's clients, who came to his office while I was working with him. While conducting business, he stopped to ask me, "Why did God say that David was a man after His own heart?"

I had to think very carefully about how to answer this question. I led him back to where David had started as a young man, raising sheep for his father, fighting and killing lions for a hobby. David was a very peculiar and special man in the sight of God. He wasn't chosen by man or in a practical way. Man sees what is on the outside, and God sees what is in our hearts.

Then I continued to explain that, as David grew up, he was like a castaway to his own family. However, in the midst of the rejection he was experiencing, something peculiar happened. The Philistines came to attack God's people, using their greatest force, led by their giant, called Goliath. Everyone was afraid of this giant, with the exception of David. He took five stones and slew the giant, to everyone's surprise, including King Saul. Thus he became a hero.

David fought many battles and won. He got messed up in his relationships and made wrong choices in his life; he was a man after God's own heart. He recognized God's sovereignty and power upon his life. He thought of God in most of his decisions and always went back to Him for forgiveness after all of his failures. He made a very sincere prayer unto God when he had committed a sin:

> Create in me a clean heart, O God,
> And renew a steadfast spirit within me.
>
> Do not cast me away from Your presence,
> And do not take Your Holy Spirit from me.
>
> Restore to me the joy of Your salvation,
> And uphold me by Your generous Spirit
> —Psalm 51:10–12

I believe that particular scripture touched the heart of God, and He forgave him. There are many other psalms written by David that clearly emphasize the sincerity of his relationship with God. Following the conversation I had with this gentleman, when I had explained the intimate connection between David and God, he immediately started to search himself about his relationship with God as a believer.

Can a believer's heart be hardened toward the things of God? Most certainly a hardened heart can be compacted with emotional baggage and heavily burdened with sinful desires. A hardened heart dulls a person's ability to perceive and understand. It can slow his mind both in the natural and supernatural. David was able to accept his failures and maintain a strong desire to change his ways.

When we refuse to wait on God and we take matters into our own hands, this is when our hearts become hardened and disordered. Mark 6:36–52 tells a great story of Jesus's miraculous work amongst his disciples and followers. Jesus went to the desert with His disciples, who had been watching Him and seeing the miracles that He performed.

When they reached the place, they realized that multitudes of people had followed Him. Feeling compassion for them, Jesus realized that the people were in need of food, and the only food available was five loaves and two fish. He blessed this and gave it to them. When they passed it around, there was a great increase in the amount of food, and it astounded the people who were there. There was even enough for them to take home.

Now it was time for the disciples to depart for their ship after the long and tiring day. Jesus went to the mountain to pray, while the others went their way. On board the ship, the disciples started to experience strong winds around them. Just around the same time, they saw a strange person walking on the sea toward the ship. Fear overtook them, and they panicked, thinking it was a ghost. Moments later they realized that it was actually Jesus, their teacher, coming to them.

With all that Jesus had done, including the healing and miracles that the disciples had experienced while with Him, they still hadn't accepted Christ fully, for their hearts were hardened. Just imagine that you have been walking around with Jesus, experiencing all the miracles, signs, and wonders, and then He goes away for a little while. All of a sudden you encounter some disturbances in your life, and you suddenly forget who you have been with. You can no longer identify the same man who walked with you before the storm approached.

This is what happens now to us; we only believe in our hearts to a limit about God whom we serve. We do not totally surrender to His command and His will; our hearts become distanced, and we begin to concentrate on the circumstances we see in the natural.

I met a woman in London when she visited our church one Sunday. Being the person I am, I went and greeted her, welcoming her to our church for the first time. I took her number and then continued to follow up with her, as our bishop had permitted me to do. She expressed her life story, telling me what she was going through, and requested counselling. When we met for our first session of analysis, she was so emotional and in pain. Her heart was hardened toward a few individuals in her family, which had resulted in hatred, unforgiveness, low self-esteem, and anger.

This sweet lady had a love for God, but she was unable to accept moving forward with a clean heart in the direction of her family. It was a painful thing to see. We talked through the areas of her hurt, and she decided to repent, release the hurts and pains from her life, and move forward with God.

A few things she mentioned that jammed in my mind were that she wanted to learn to love again, she wanted to love herself unconditionally, and she wanted to be wiser in choosing her friends and relationships. I was intrigued to know that she wanted to learn to love herself, and that really struck a chord in me. There are many people we meet who appear to be okay. They smile and they communicate effectively with other people, but they are experiencing major problems within themselves.

Many times we don't know how to love ourselves, and therefore it becomes very hard to love others. Acceptance is the crucial fact here; we place limits and demands on our lives, thinking that things must take a certain approach at all times. There are people all over the place going about not knowing who they are or what their purpose is.

Some of them were not accepted by their parents and were not shown how to love or show compassion. Their hearts become tough, with no empathy concerning other people and no room to forgive. This is the reason why Christ came! He came for the weak, the lonely, the unloved, the broken, and the hopeless.

Christ will always be there when the storm comes. When you are burdened, He will give you rest; when you have trouble on every side, He will be your deliverer; when you are sick, He will become your healer; when you are unloved, He will show love and compassion; when you have low self-esteem, He will tell you how special you are; and when you are angry, He will help you demonstrate kindness. One of the greatest things anyone could ever do for us on this earth, Christ did. He died for our sins so that we have redemption through His blood.

> For God so loved the world that He gave His
> only begotten Son, that whoever believes in Him
> should not perish but have everlasting life.
> —John 3:16

This was the greatest love ever written about in history, and God demonstrated that to us. Therefore we have an example to follow. We have sinned so many times in our lives, but God, in His mercy, through his son Jesus Christ, forgave us and continues to have compassion on us.

When our hearts are not right with God, He still loves us. When we mess up, he still shows us His unconditional love in more ways than one. Today, this very minute, God's desire is to have our hearts, my friend. So ask him to remove the stony heart—yes, the hardened heart—and to give you a heart of flesh so that you'll be strengthened to receive His boundless love to pursue His will. This will enable you to accept others in love and sympathy, not rendering evil in exchange for evil.

We need to disperse the evil thoughts, the damages and

troubles, the challenging memories of the past, the abuse and violence, the bad habits and hatred, the anger, envy, jealousy, and pride. We need to walk away from those sinful behaviors and begin to embrace the love of God today in our hearts. Then we can be at liberty.

The Bible teaches and emphasizes that forgiveness of sin and healing of the body go hand in hand. God aspires to heal our temperaments through His word. While in London, I was privileged to be in a counselling class where I was taught how to deal with individuals and their situations. I learned to help others—but at the end I also found out more about myself. I discovered that there are five different temperaments that pinpoint our perception of ourselves and the people who love us. Temperament is also a determining factor in how well we handle the stresses and pressures of life.

Temperament can best be defined as spiritual genetics or God's imprint upon each one of us. These involve the conception of a child, the mother, the father, and the Creator. These temperaments are described as melancholic, choleric, sanguine, phlegmatic, and supine.

These are inborn—not about genetics or your inherited genes but the natural parts of man that determine how you react to people, places, and things. In other words, it's not the people you hang out with but simply the way you react with your environment and the world around you.

David talked in scriptures about the way God designed us before we were born (Psalm 139:13–16 NIV). "For you created my inmost being; you knit me together in my mother's womb.

"I praise you because I am fearfully and wonderfully made; your works are wonderful, I know that full well. My frame was not hidden from you when I was made in the secret place. When I was woven together in the depths of the earth, your eyes saw my unformed body. All the days ordained for me were written in your book before one of them come to be."

In this psalm David clearly stated that God knew us long before we knew ourselves. We are specially designed the way we are only by the order of God. When we were born, there were certain things we were not taught by our parents (i.e., how to cry and to know when we are hungry); we each had a personality, a character, and temperament.

When you see someone acting a certain way, don't judge him or her based on what you see, but get to understand the person and work with him or her. God placed a certain unique temperament in each of us, and the behavior we display is strongly affected by the environment we associate ourselves in and which allows us to see, hear, smell, feel, and learn.

Our behavior permits us to understand and select our own way of doing things. We display our personalities and express ourselves in the way we know how in order to survive in the world.

If we as ministers would teach the gospel of Jesus Christ, people would have faith in the word of God for their healing and receiving forgiveness. Then, also, sinners would come to the truth and be converted by the teaching of the word. The word of God is to be taught to the people in order to change their hearts.

The following scriptures prove that both benefits were provided in the sacrifice of Christ on Calvary. Jesus Christ took our infirmities and bore our sicknesses (Matthew 8:16–17).

> Who Himself bore our sins in His own
> body on the tree, that we, having died
> to sins, might live for righteousness—
> by whose stripes you were healed.
> —1 Peter 2:24

Sicknesses come in many different forms, one of which can affect the heart.

Who forgives all your iniquities,
Who heals all your diseases?
—Psalm 103:3

The following scriptures prove that forgiveness of sins and healing of the body should be received at one time.

For which is easier, to say, "Your sins are
forgiven you," or to say, "Arise and walk"?
—Matthew 9:5

For the hearts of this people have grown dull.
Their ears are hard of hearing,
And their eyes they have closed,
Lest they should see with their eyes
and hear with their ears,
Lest they should understand
with their hearts and turn,
So that I should heal them.
—Matthew 13:15

Is anyone among you sick? Let him call for the
elders of the church, and let them pray over
him, anointing him with oil in the name of the
Lord. And the prayer of faith will save the sick,
and the Lord will raise him up. And if he has
committed sins, he will be forgiven. Confess
your trespasses to one another, and pray for one
another, that you may be healed. The effective,
fervent prayer of a righteous man avails much.
–James 5:14–16

It is a clear depiction showing us that healing is just as easy to receive from God as forgiveness of sins. Both can be received by simple faith in God and asking in the name of Jesus. Healing belongs to us; it's our salvation through Jesus Christ. Do not allow yourself to be cheated out of it any more than you permitted yourself to be robbed out of forgiveness of sins.

I visited a friend's home after she had been discharged prematurely from the hospital, having had a difficult time giving birth to her second child. She was so sick that she was unable to do anything for herself. I watched her as she lay in bed in excruciating pain. I was unhappy to see my friend so helpless; I wanted to do something for her and did not know what to do. We agreed to pray together, as I was alone in her bedroom with her at that time. Her feet were swollen, and it seemed as if they were about to pop open.

As I write about it, I can vividly picture everything in my mind; it's a sight I will not forget anytime soon. I straightaway went onto my knees at the end of her bed, and I began to pray. I called on the angels of heaven to come forth, as it was an emergency situation for my friend. The doctors had not done what they were supposed to have done, which had led to her condition. However, I strongly believed that God was allowing my friend to go through this process for a reason.

That was God's proof, as part of her journey experience and to let the doctors know that He was still the miraculous God, the One who never fails. She was a committed woman of God whom He was developing for a remarkable ministry, needed at this time for broken women and those who had been through similar circumstances. That was the task, God's purpose, she was being called to fulfill on earth.

As I began praying, her faith started to extend, and together we believed God would heal her. She believed in the God of miracles and accepted her healing immediately. God can do anything for you. If you have need of healing, He will heal you. It is only right that you surrender your life to God, and He will take care of you. You will not only receive your healing but you will be freed and will obtain salvation (if you are not already saved) from the sinful lifestyles of this world.

After we'd prayed and I had left, a midwife who is our bishop's wife happened to be in the area and stopped by to see her. She advised my friend to go to the hospital immediately. Without hesitation her husband took her to the hospital, where they admitted her right away as an emergency case. Later on the doctors recognized their negligence for discharging her earlier without sufficient examination.

We thanked God for His divine intervention—He showed up on time and aided her. She was totally healed and was listed as a miracle woman, leaving the physicians in shock over the healing touch of God. Now she has an amazing testimony to share with the world.

The point I want to emphasize here is that faith in God works—if you can only believe that the God who raised Jesus from the dead is the same God who reigns today in our lives.

There is nothing that is impossible for God to do. If it's cancer, you can be healed, whatever your diagnosis is. God can and He will deliver you, if you only believe. If you will ask God for healing of the body, mind, and soul, and believe that it is done—in exactly the same way that we are taught to ask for forgiveness of sins—whatever it might be, it will be accomplished.

We should not doubt that God can and will heal us and set us free. Just as we are trained to believe in the pardon of sins, we have been taught that God forgives us regardless of our feelings and that if we will believe this, we will be saved. Thus it is with healing of the body. After prayer has been completed and healing has been asked for, we should likewise count it done and believe it, irrespective of our feelings, symptoms, or outward evidence to the contrary.

CHAPTER 14

Prayer Is the Key

We all need someone to encourage us in prayer. I recall a couple who loved the Lord and always did whatever they could to live a life that pleased Him. The woman was a very outspoken person, but the husband was a man of few words.

They prayed and made plans to start having children. Not long afterward, the woman became pregnant, and they were grateful to God. They followed every medical step to make sure that a healthy child was born. The big day came, and the husband got the wife to the hospital to deliver the baby. Throughout her pregnancy everything with the baby had been normal, which was good news for the family.

Finally the baby came, and that was a joyful moment. However, the following morning the attending doctor came to the woman's room and sat down to talk with her. What the doctor said was very discouraging—heartbreaking news. The doctor said, "Something is wrong with the baby." Not only that, but he told her the baby would have to be airlifted to another hospital many miles away for immediate surgery. Just before the doctor left the room, the woman's husband entered and received the news as well. It was a very difficult thing for them to deal with.

Then all kinds of thoughts started to run through their minds, and the woman was broken. *Does God really care about us going through this? Is God seeing what is happening to our dear baby? Why did this happen at all?* These were the woman's questions.

Then the husband, he who normally didn't talk much, grabbed the wife's hands and started to pray. He said, "God, thank you for this child you have given us. He is actually yours, not ours, and so we leave him in your hands, because he belongs to you. Whatever is going on with him right now, you know it all, so be with him when we can't, in Jesus's name. Amen." The normally outspoken women was quiet, but this time God was using the husband, giving him the strength to encourage her when her heart was broken, her spirit crushed, and her faith gone.

God surely knows His children and cares for them. At times when we feel as if no one is around, or no one cares, or no one hears, and there is no one to help, at the right and perfect time God shows up, according to His will, plan, and purpose.

If we will mention that we are healed just as much as we are forgiven, God will confirm and manifest the healing, just as He does forgiveness of sins. This fact cannot be overemphasized—healing depends much on this secure stand that prayer has been heard and answered. If you want to acquire these benefits, then you will not fail to obtain them. It is not always guaranteed, according to the word of God, that you will benefit from everything that you ask, but all is based on His will and purpose for you.

Is it worth it? Are these benefits worth the efforts of being submissive and obedient to God? If they are, then the effort will be beneficial as long as the instructions are followed.

There are times we find it so difficult to follow instructions, but in the long run we want to enjoy the benefits. The key here is to believe God without doubting or being indecisive about having faith and obeying His commands. If and when we decide to believe, then it will be unnecessary to worry.

How can we expect God to honor His word and give us what

we desire if we do not surrender to Him, as required of us? He is no respecter of person. He is not a man or the type of god that will break His laws in order to compromise with individuals. God knows His people; He knows the thoughts of everyone from far off. He knows that all of us could make that effort, if we would only try as hard as we can to have unwavering faith.

Do not engage in self-pity any longer or complain that it is difficult to believe. This kind of behavior is ranked as sinful, and therefore the way forward is to ask for God's forgiveness of the lies. The enemy will always tempt us to believe other than the truth of our Lord and Savior. As long as we are cooperating with the enemy, Satan, and allowing unbelief and sinful desires to tarnish our lives, we will be unable to cooperate with God and practice the true faith. It is not recommended to serve two masters or have faith and unbelief walking hand in hand. Reflect on Matthew 6:24 and James. 1:4–8, and choose Christ's pathway. Live for Him daily, and He will perfect His will in your life.

As you have read in previous paragraphs, it is God's will to heal, because He has definitely promised to heal all who come to Him in faith. It is not a good thing to question God or make Him a liar. God has guaranteed healing for us and reassured us in His word; therefore it is sinful to doubt His promises.

God's will is not an opinion, statement, or revelation. It is revealed through His words, and there is no need to seek it anywhere else. His words are final and cannot change for any situation.

The Holy Spirit is key here. He will continue to reveal God's will and guide you on your journey toward your breakthrough. According to John 16:13–14, we all need the Holy Spirit.

> For as many as are led by the Spirit
> of God, these are sons of God.
> —Romans 8:14

The Holy Spirit works on our behalf. Before Jesus left the earth, He said that He would send the comforter, the Holy Spirit, who would guide us unto all truth. The truth is that we cannot be independent of the Spirit of God. He corrects, He directs, He inspires, and He reveals.

A friend of mine who lived in London had been through great pain and sorrow with the loss of two family members. I can recall it as vividly as if it were yesterday. This lady had a sister who had suffered from the deadly disease cancer. She had watched her sister suffer through the pain and discomfort. Days went by as we'd prayed and believed God for her healing and as we kept the faith in the word of God.

We could not understand how a healthy woman could get sick one day, and in spite of the prayers and the fasting, she was just fading right before our eyes. The day she passed we were all saddened by the fact that God had decided to take this talented woman of God away from her family and friends.

A few years after this lady lost her sister, her mum had also died; she had suffered the same sickness. How much more could this lady bear? Her family was slowly being taken away from her. People wondered, *Why do these things happen to God's people? Did we doubt? Was it the will of God for this lady to go through such pain?* No one knows the plans of God; even when we pray and believe in His word.

God will answer anyone who quits doubting His word and His will and prays in faith according to the promises. Just imagine for a moment if the Holy Spirit were to say to someone, "Do not go to work today. Stay in, and get some rest." But the individual begins to think about his employer and about losing out on getting paid for that day, so he ignores the voice speaking and decides to go nonetheless.

This is considered to be disobedience to the voice of the Holy Spirit, leaving the house despite the warning signals. Now suppose an unfortunate accident happens on the way, and the person loses a leg or maybe dies. Do you think it was the will of God for such misfortune to happen? The answer is no. The key point is that obedience to God's voice works hand in hand with the will of God and the direction of the Holy Spirit when He speaks.

From the foundation of the earth, it was God's will for man to live, not die, whether it be physical death or spiritual death. On the other hand, because of the sinful nature of man, sickness and death continue to occur. Praise be to God that man has been redeemed by the blood of the lamb.

Christ died so that these sins can be remitted to help us achieve eternal life. What an awesome feeling it is to know that we can go to God through His son, Jesus, for healing and deliverance. It takes much seeking, by praying and believing that God can restore us back to good health. No matter what the doctors say or do, God's word is final. Hence we have confidence in the word in spite of what a report may say. God's word declares that we are free.

When we communicate with God by using His word back to Him, it will not return unto him void but accomplish what it was planned to do. Prayer is powerful; prayer is a means of communication, bringing back His word to Him for confirmation and response. If we have been brought up under the authority of Christ and the Bible, however, we should know that God wills for us to pray. We now know that His will is good and perfect for us.

Don't believe that prayer is an impersonal requirement. We must realize that God is a person, the Lord Jesus Christ, with all power, authority, and love. He expects us to pray. The scriptures below show us clearly that He expects us to pray: Matthew 6:5–7,

Matthew 6:9, Luke 11:9, Luke 18:1. It is demonstrated by our *asking,* *seeking,* and *knocking*—this forms the acronym ASK.

What if Jesus should appear to you personally, just as He did to the apostle John on the Isle of Patmos, which is listed in the book of Revelation 1? It declares that He expects us to pray. Wouldn't you become more faithful in prayer? Would you not speak to God regularly? Whether you are in need of something or not, this means just knowing that Jesus expects you to pray at all times. The word of Jesus, quoted in the scriptures above, confirms His will for us in the same aspect as if we were face to face and He was speaking to us. There are times when we will rely on someone if something happens to us, just to receive that nudge to seek God in prayer.

Yes, we need individuals to intercede on our behalf, but most importantly we need that bond of communication with God, our master. We don't need to be professionals in praying; it's not the elaborate words or the length of the prayer. It's the effectiveness and consistency of seeking the Lord that is important, and also praying back His word to Him, which will not return unto Him empty.

According to Colossians 4:2, we should devote ourselves to prayer. Everyone is devoted to something; most of us are devoted to many things, which can sometimes cause distraction. When we make a priority, or sacrifice for it, or give time to it, then we know we are devoted to it. God expects Christians to be devoted to prayer and the word of God.

> Pray without ceasing.
> —1 Thessalonians 5:17

When we offer ourselves to prayer, it places emphasis on the prayer as an activity. Therefore, when we pray continually it should develop us and help us to know that prayer is also a relationship. It also can be noted as an expression of a Christian's loving relationship with our heavenly Father.

Praying without ceasing or praying continually doesn't mean that we do nothing but pray. The word of God expects many other things from us besides prayer, including times of rest when we cannot consciously pray. But it does mean that if talking and thinking of God can't be in the forefront of our minds, it should always be peeking over and ready to take the place of what we are concentrating on.

The enemy will consistently bring distractions our way that cause us to be less focused on our communication with God. It could be a phone call, a spouse, our children, etc. However, God needs us to set aside the things that will cause distraction. He wants our full attention, because when we pray, we need to focus and believe in what we are praying for so that we will receive answers. We often pray in error, and the thing we ask God for we don't receive. Does that mean God is punishing us for not having enough faith to believe what we pray for?

While I was in Jamaica and going through a transition period, I was able to meet a few people whom I hadn't seen for over fifteen years. I saw some of the friends I grew up with in church; we'd attended Sunday school, sang in the choir, and even attended the same school together. This was an experience I will never forget. During the process, I discovered that one of my friends was ill and requesting to see me.

I'd known this friend for many years, and now I discovered that she'd been diagnosed with cancer. Considering her condition, I was hesitant to visit straightaway, because I personally felt unprepared. One of the reasons was that I didn't know what to expect. I didn't know how to minister to her based on the report I'd seen. It was a real challenge for me when I went to her house and met her beautiful children and husband for the very first time.

It was very apparent that they had a wonderful relationship as a family. As I entered the room and saw her lying on her bed, my heart was in pain. An instant feeling of anger struck me. I couldn't understand why people had to suffer the way they did. This deadly disease had attacked another servant of God. I started ministering to my friend before praying. I was able to understand her strong faith and the relationship she had with God as well as the trust she had in him to deliver her from her infirmities.

There was a strong energy of fear in the room. Even though she believed in the word of God and His power, the atmosphere was still challenging for a breakthrough in prayer. James 5:14–16 states, "Is any sick among you? Let him call for the elders of the church, and let them pray over him, anointing him with oil in the name of the Lord Jesus, and the prayer of faith shall save the sick."

> And these signs will follow those who believe:
> In My name they will cast out demons; they
> will speak with new tongues; they will take up
> serpents; and if they drink anything deadly,
> it will by no means hurt them; they will lay
> hands on the sick, and they will recover.
> So then, after the Lord had spoken to them,
> He was received up into heaven, and sat
> down at the right hand of God. And they
> went out and preached everywhere, the Lord
> working with them and confirming the word
> through the accompanying signs. Amen.
> —Mark 16:17–20

I requested the anointing oil, and then I prayed over it. Then I asked her to believe in God with me, because He has the power to heal the sick, no matter what the conditions, and not by me laying hands on her for healing. Without the power of God working in me I am nothing but simply a tool, only to be used by God. At that point, I still sensed the fear and disbelief in the atmosphere. You can say you believe from your mouth, but your heart may not be totally in sync with what you say. This happens to us all the time.

As I anointed her with the oil, I believed in my heart that God would heal her, and I prayed for her very intensely. There was also another person in the room who believed in God as I prayed. I had confidence in God's healing any form of disease. There is nothing too difficult for God to do; all we need to do is activate our faith to receive our healing and deliverance. After praying and leaving the house, I knew in my heart that God had started the healing process. All my friend needed to do was to build up her faith in the word and to trust God. Before leaving, I gave her a few scriptures to reflect upon.

We continued to pray and believe in God for complete healing. I heard reports that she was feeling stronger and was able to do some things she hadn't been able to do before. Another time there were reports that she was not doing well. It continued for a little while, and then one morning I got the news that she had passed away. Were the prayers not effective, or was there not enough faith for her to receive her total healing?

Only God knew the outcome of this situation. For us, it was so sudden to lose a friend that way. We had all prayed, including the church members, the family, and friends, but the prayers hadn't been answered the way we wanted. What had gone wrong? Did it mean that God doesn't answer prayers? No! He still answers prayers; He is not a man, that he should lie. He is faithful in all His promises. He is the healer, He is God, and nothing changes. People get upset with God when things don't happen the way they want them to. We might lose someone very close to us, or we might lose our jobs, but whatever it is, remember this: God's promise for His children never changes.

It is our duty to pray and believe what God says He will do through His word. According to Martin Luther, who was a praying man as well as a reformer of the church, "As is the business of tailors to make clothes and cobblers to make shoes, so it is the business of Christians to pray."

However, we must expect to pray not only as a divine summons but also as a royal invitation. God is inviting us to come in and stay in—in the Holies of Holies, where we will experience change.

> Let us therefore come boldly to the throne
> of grace, that we may obtain mercy and
> find grace to help in time of need.
> —Hebrews 4:16

We can be prayer pessimists and see the expectation to pray merely as obligation, or we can be optimists who view the command to pray as an opportunity to receive the mercy and grace of God.

My darling husband Charles expects from me a call when I go out, to let him know that I have reached my destination. I will also call to let him know when I'm leaving to come back home. This is an expectation between us, an expectation of love and communication. He advises that I call because he wants to hear that I have had a safe journey. Our God's expectation of us is that we pray to Him.

His command for us to pray is a command of love. In His love He desires to communicate with us and bless us. Just as in the army, when the commander expects to hear from the solders on the battlefield, God expects us to pray to Him. One writer reminds us that "Prayer is a walkie-talkie for warfare, not a domestic intercom for increasing our convenience."

God expects us to use the walkie-talkie, prayer, because it is the means He has ordained not only for godliness but also for the spiritual warfare between His kingdom and the kingdom of His enemy. To abandon prayer is to fight the battle with only our own resources at best and to lose interest in the battle at worse.

Now, we know that sometimes when we pray and ask God for something it takes a great activeness of faith that touches the heart of God. It's not the will of God for man to be sick to death; we must use this walkie-talkie of prayer and faith, understand the season we are in, and pray effectively. Please note that Jesus didn't heal everyone. Some had to die, while others had to go through the process to receive their healing.

The story of the woman with the issue of blood is listed in the Gospel of Luke 8:43–48, and it is also recorded in other gospels. This woman tried everything she possibly could to get her healing. The doctors couldn't heal her, and she spent all that she had in her desperation to receive healing. She sought for twelve years; the Bible was specific on the number of years she had been suffering.

A number of people might have advised her to give up because there was no hope. She would probably have given up at one point in her life; but then she heard of a man called Jesus who had been healing and delivering people. This might have been her final hope of ever receiving her healing, and so straightaway she obtained hope again.

You may have heard people say, "How can I believe it when I don't see it? If I could only see it or feel it, then I could believe that something is happening!"

The woman with the issue of blood who came to Jesus could have felt the same way. For twelve long years she had gone from one doctor to another, trying every conceivable cure they could offer. She did not only get worse but ended up losing all her resources.

Then something happened to her, when "she heard about Jesus" (Mark 5:27). She started believing that He could and would heal her, to the extent that she said, "If only I may touch His clothes, I shall be made well" (Mark 5:28). Acting on her belief, she made her way to the area where Jesus was and managed to touch His garment. Immediately her bleeding stopped, and she felt in her body that she was healed of that affliction. Jesus, her true physician, also pronounced her healed.

The woman understood that this was her season of breakthrough. She'd found out that He was coming to town, so she'd prepared herself the best way she could, even though her condition was embarrassing. No matter how shameful your condition might be, when you are desperate for something, nothing else matters. Obviously, she did not care what the crowd was saying; she was anxious to obtain her healing.

On that day, I can only imagine the thousands of people who had gathered to meet Jesus: the sick, the lame, the blind, and those who were on the verge of dying. The atmosphere must have been tense. This woman didn't watch what was happening, and she wasn't afraid of the commotion at that moment.

Since she was in a frantic situation, she didn't think about humiliation or the way people would react when they saw her approaching Jesus. This woman was scorned by many individuals because her issue was obvious to the crowd, but she still pressed her way through to receive her victory. The crowd was so big that she was unable to see the face of Jesus. She knew He was there, and so this time she could feel His presence.

She pushed and pushed until she was able to touch the hem of Jesus's garment, and instantaneously she was made whole—she was completely healed of her infirmity. Her faith was extended so much that Jesus asked, "Who touched me?"

The disciples did not understand the kind of touch Jesus was making reference to, and they replied, "But Master, there are a lot of people touching you. How can you ask such a question?" But Jesus repeated the same question: "Who touched me?" Christ felt a touch of faith, the touch that only He could identify. This touch of desperation and determination can embody the act of faith that signifies the power of no surrender.

Desperation and faith bring results. Whenever you decide to push, no matter what the consequences, pray and seek God while

He may be found. This lady believed that if she could only touch something of Jesus's, it really didn't matter what, she would be cured.

The Bible said, "Immediately as she touched Him she was made whole." She pulled virtue, power, and the anointing from Him. That moment was her season for breakthrough, because she believed. The lady understood that her season had come, and so without hesitation she pushed, pressed, and prayed until she received what was hers.

Beloved, God wants you to know that when you believe Him you will see your miracle. That which you believe in Him for you will receive. Let no one shorten your belief in what God can miraculously do for you through His Son, Jesus Christ.

It's time to understand your season and begin to launch into it. You cannot dwell on what you see, because sometimes you will only see failure and disappointment, which invite the negativity in your heart. If you speak negatively over the issues in your life, you will shut down the ability to achieve your goals and your deliverance. In this life good things don't just happen when we want them to; we must have faith to know that they can occur.

Hebrews 11:1 tells us, "Now faith is the substance of things hoped for, the evidence of things not seen." Many people are challenged by this scripture. It can be difficult to believe when certain situations arise.

Then "what if …" comes to haunt us and make us embrace doubt in our minds, which causes us to lose focus on God's word. These little words can be taunting to the natural mind; that's why it's important to have our minds firmly fitted in Him.

Our minds can be spiritual battlefields. We keep on fighting and resisting the truth of God's word and build a blockage to belief when it's convenient to do so. Note that the abovementioned woman did not speak a word to Jesus. She had done enough talking through her process of getting her healing. Sometimes we use our mouths unwisely and block our blessings from God.

Our confrontations can be dangerous to us; there are times when we have to speak out and other times when it's essential for us to act upon what we have learned. It's all about control—we often let our tongues get out of control as we express words of unbelief and negativity; this results in disappointment when we desire to have success.

There is one who speaks like
the piercings of a sword,
But the tongue of the wise promotes health.
—Proverbs 12:18

He who guards his mouth preserves his life,
But he who opens wide his lips
shall have destruction.
—Proverbs 13:3

A wholesome tongue is a tree of life,
But perverseness in it breaks the spirit.
—Proverbs 15:4

There is a way that seems right to a man,
But its end is the way of death.
—Proverbs 16:25

Death and life are in the power of the tongue,
And those who love it will eat its fruit.
—Proverbs 18:21

We must therefore resist the danger of the tongue, for when we do not put it under serious subjection it causes us to fail. We should be able to speak the word of life over ourselves to become free. Words are indeed powerful and sharper than any two-edged sword. Many individuals find themselves in serious dilemmas because of what comes out of their mouths. Our words become unprotected, especially if they include negativity. We should practice to use our tongues wisely concerning what we declare in the lives of others.

This works both ways. As we expect people to do to us, we should do the same to them. We should make it our duty to protect one another with words of life, not death. The scripture reveals that death and life are in the power of the tongue, which means that when you speak into someone's life, you must be very careful what you say. Speak life and help someone to prosper. Avoid gossip; otherwise it will lead you down the wrong pathway of life.

> For he who would love life
> And see good days,
> Let him refrain his tongue from evil,
> And his lips from speaking deceit.
> —1 Peter 3:10

Whenever you misuse your mouth, especially using it as a defense, it can easily cause danger—not only to yourself but to those around you. Let the words of your mouth and the meditation of your heart be acceptable in the sight of God.

It is important to ponder on the things that are good so that you can exercise protecting each other. You are your brothers' keeper; therefore it is required that you have a solid foundation to build on. When you are living for Christ, you are expected to follow practical rules, according to the word of God.

These protocols include living and breathing the words, fulfilling His commands, abiding in His laws, and standing for righteousness. Where are you now in your walk with God? Are you indecisive about who to serve and how to live a holy life? Are you struggling to be committed to Him and remain righteous and faithful? Are you confused about where to start and how to get this right?

One of my favorite psalms in the Bible is Psalm 91; it is the perfect place to live and remain stable. I always remind myself that this scripture is for me. It has become my home; it's where I desire to be. It has become my security, shelter and, most of all, my protection. When you live for God and remain under His protection, you will know that you are secure and sheltered by Him from the hazards the enemy places in your way.

Just picture yourself walking in the rain without an umbrella; you become exposed to the rain. But when you are sheltered under an umbrella, you are protected from the rain. Another example is the protection a hen gives her newly hatched chicks. She always keeps a guard on the chicks to ensure that they are secured under her wings, keeping them away from predators. Jesus's arms are always stretched out, welcoming us to stay under His protection, but there are times when we walk out from under His covering.

CHAPTER 15

THE POWER OF PRAYER

He who dwells in the secret
place of the Most High
Shall abide under the shadow of the Almighty.
I will say of the LORD, "He is my
refuge and my fortress;
My God, in Him I will trust." Surely He shall
deliver you from the snare of the fowler
And from the perilous pestilence.
He shall cover you with His feathers,
And under His wings you shall take refuge;
His truth shall be your shield and buckler.
You shall not be afraid of the terror by night,
Nor of the arrow that flies by day,
Nor of the pestilence that walks in darkness,
Nor of the destruction that
lays waste at noonday.

A thousand may fall at your side,
And ten thousand at your right hand;
But it shall not come near you.

Only with your eyes shall you look,
And see the reward of the wicked. Because
you have made the LORD, who is my refuge,
Even the Most High, your dwelling place,
No evil shall befall you,
Nor shall any plague come near your dwelling;
For He shall give His angels charge over you,
To keep you in all your ways.
In their hands they shall bear you up,
Lest you dash your foot against a stone.
You shall tread upon the lion and the cobra,
The young lion and the serpent
you shall trample underfoot.

"Because he has set his love upon
Me, therefore I will deliver him;
I will set him on high, because
he has known My name.
He shall call upon Me, and I will answer him;
I will be with him in trouble;
I will deliver him and honor him.
With long life I will satisfy him,
And show him My salvation."

—Psalm 91

To exemplify the rule of the ninety-first Psalm, I relate the following story. This happened in London, at my previous place of employment. I worked with children in a day-care nursery, where I managed eight staff members and approximately sixty children. It was a challenge for me, but I loved my job. It was a setting that encouraged different cultures and religions. I tried not to interfere with other people's beliefs and the gods they served. I knew that the god I served was a true and living god.

My ministry is to serve and introduce the word of God. I can boast and testify of the miracle-working God I have a relationship with. Everyone in the setting at that time knew my beliefs and that there were certain customs and beliefs I would not partake in. There were teachers from various religious backgrounds, including Christian and other.

Every year the children had the opportunity to celebrate their faith, according to the curriculum. It was around the time for certain religious sects to celebrate their big holiday and therefore time to display their religious props in the building. At this time of the year I tried not to partake, and I also surrounded my work area with the blood of Jesus each morning when I prayed.

Some of my co-workers were responsible for the display. They collected items from their homes and the community to make the scenery. They made a huge display; I was astounded when I saw it. As I walked in that morning, the images I saw were beyond my description. The display was to be in a designated are, where it was clearly visible for everyone entering the building for the celebration. My initial thought was to pray and plead the blood of Jesus Christ to cover the children and staff as well as anyone entering the building, since from my point of view it looked very strange.

I was disturbed and unhappy by what I saw, and I went immediately to my office, as I felt uncomfortable in that atmosphere. My workplace was like a second home to me. I was always there when the children came in and out. I provided a surrounding for them where they were able to express themselves freely; therefore, the setting was like a second home as well. I came out of my office to use the restroom, the entrance of which was located next to the display. On the other side was the entrance to the children's toilet area. While I was in the restroom, I decided to pray one more time. This time I was almost directly in the display area.

My spirit was grieved, and I wasn't settled at all. While praying, I began to bind up every unclean spirit that had entered the setting and prayed that the Holy Spirit would take over and saturate the place with the blood of Jesus and allow His presence to be our dwelling place. I spoke the word of God back to Him and included Psalm 91 in my prayer.

It is important to know that we have the power of Jesus Christ in us through His undiluted word, which was written to be our guideline. I went back to my office feeling a sense of release from the atmosphere. A few hours later, I was called out of my office by a staff member, who was reporting an incident that had taken place in the children's toilet area.

It was reported that a child had gone to the restroom and, after washing hands, mistakenly left the tap water running, causing an overflow. The sink was flooded, and the strangest thing happened. The water flooded the toilet area, came streaming around the area of the display, and washed away everything that was present for the celebrations.

Who could it have been but Jesus? *No evil shall come near our dwelling.* I declared the word of God, and it proved His power one more time to me. Those who were around could not understand how it could have happened the way it did, but I knew about the power of God. I went into my office and started rejoicing, giving thanks and praise to God for the victory. This experience taught me that all things are possible to those who believe. On many occasions since then, if I only believed, I have experienced and proved the promises of God and found them to be steadfast in His will.

For all the promises of God in Him are Yes, and
in Him Amen, to the glory of God through us.
—2 Corinthians 1:20

I grew up understanding the importance of prayer. As an intercessor, my aim is to always remain connected to God and seek His face. One of the most sacred and intimate times to be in the company of the Holy Spirit is in the early morning prayer time, which I found effective, for then you are not easily disturbed while you are in His presence.

Continuous prayer and waiting on God will result in breakthrough, even though it is not always easy to remain committed. The moment you dedicate your time to something you will follow through. Amidst any hardship you may experience, if you hold on you will benefit greatly—it's all about perseverance and faith. Since prayer is expected of every believer, will you pray? Will you take that attitude today and journey through the pathway of prayer?

I challenge you with this directly, because I think we all need to make some conscious decisions about our prayer life. It's time for general intentions about prayer to become the specific plans of our lives.

A pastor who agreed with the above statement emphasized the following: "Unless I'm badly mistaken, one of the main reasons so many of God's children don't have a significant prayer life is not so much that we don't want to but that we don't plan to. If you want to take a four-week vacation, you don't just get up one summer running and say; "Hey, let's go today!" You won't have anything ready. You know where to go, but nothing has been planned. Yet that is how many of us treat prayer! We don't know where to go. Nothing has been planned—no time, place, or procedure—and we all know that the opposite of planning does not result in a wonderful flow of deep, spontaneous prayer experience.

The opposite of having a plan is being disorganized. If you don't plan a vacation you will probably stay home and watch TV, which is the natural. When the flow of spiritual life is unplanned, it sinks to the lowest receding tide of vitality. There is a race to run and a fight to be fought. If you want renewal in your life of prayer, you must plan to see it.

Therefore, for the purpose of godliness, will you pray today? Will you plan to pray tomorrow? The days after that, will you just pray? Learn it, practice it, live it, and most of all, be committed to it. Prayer is the key to every situation in the Christian's life. For that reason, come and pledge your life to total prayer. Have you ever gotten involved in something in your life that you will never bounce back from because of the scars and pains you incurred in the process? Have you asked yourself, *Can I get back to that place where I don't need to worry about anything in my life? Does life have to be a struggle at all times? Why do other people in the world seem to be at a better place than I am now in my life?* These questions continue to plague our minds every day. The answers will bring us to the knowledge that prayer is the key and that it generates the power of God through His word.

CHAPTER 16

MARRED FOR PROCESSING

Struggles, traumas, abuse (physical, emotional, sexual, and spiritual), deaths, job issues, homelessness, financial struggles, mental issues—the list could go further. We all have something to testify about.

We all are experiencing something one way or the other. A friend of mine often says that "every home has it"—every home is experiencing a situation that only through God's intervention can the people survive. Has your home been affected to some degree by the enemy's devices to cause hurt and pain? If that's the case, I'm here to tell you that the restorer is here. Jesus is on the scene to deliver you from your difficulties.

I want to attract your attention to the story of Job. Job was a faithful and committed man of God who had everything a person could want and more. He had the perfect family, livestock, lands, plantations, and houses. You name it, he had it all. As his story continues, he lost all he had through no fault of his own. He struggled to understand why this had happened to him. Just as we find it hard to comprehend the things that happen to us in this life, it became clear that he wasn't meant to know the reasons for the misfortune. It was for God's glory.

Can we learn to trust God the way Job did? Or will we choose to give in to temptation by the enemy and then say that God really didn't care at all: "He just allowed these things to happen to me; why should I trust him or serve him?"

God wants the best for us; no matter what things may seem like, this is always the final truth. He allows certain things to happen so that we can learn to trust faithfully without doubting in the process. Job chapters 1 and 2 begin to tell you the story of a man who knew the God he served separately from his enemy. He stood for every godly principle, no matter what the critics, the accusers, and the advisers said.

Let's look again at Job. He was a very wealthy man who owned much land and livestock; he was married and had ten children (Job 1:1–5 NIV). "In the land of UZ there lived a man whose name was Job. This man was blameless and upright; he feared God and shunned evil.

"He had seven sons and three daughters, and he owned seven thousand sheep, three thousand camels, five hundred yoke of oxen, and five thousand donkeys, and had a large number of servants. He was the greatest man among all the people of the east."

His sons used to take turns holding feasts in their homes, and they would invite their three sisters to eat and drink with them. When a period of feasting had run its course, Job would have them purified. Early in the mornings he would sacrifice a burnt offering for each of them thinking, *Perhaps my children have sinned and cursed God in their hearts.* This was Job's regular custom.

He wasn't in need of anything, and most importantly, he served God faithfully. He had made sacrifices unto God and had committed all his children to God; they all knew the relationship their dad had with his God.

When you are connected to God fully and living righteously, He will take care of you. Remember that God never goes back on His word. Nevertheless, the enemy is waiting for the right chance to attack you; he's anticipating an opportunity to devour you in a test of faith in your God.

The Bible says that there was a day when all the angels gathered themselves at the throne of God, and guess who showed up? It was Satan, the enemy of mankind. And God asked him, "So, what are you here for? Where have you come from?"

Satan's reply was, "From roaming through the earth and going back and forth in it." Satan, our enemy, goes to and fro around the earth seeking whom he may devour.

He prowls around to deceive, to lie, to steal, to kill, and to destroy God's children. We need to be sober, vigilant, and on the alert. We should not take sickness and disease carelessly or take sudden attacks in an ordinary manner, because there is an evil force working against us.

But we can be thankful that we are connected to a higher source, who has all the power to deliver and set us free. Now God said to Satan, "Have you considered my servant Job?" Verse 8 of chapter 1 says, "There is no one on earth like him; he is blameless and upright, a man who fears God and shuns evil."

How amazing it is that God gave such a profound account about Job. God knew about Job's lifestyle and all that he was capable of doing.

The God we serve is mindful of every situation we face in life. He's aware of the things we do and say; when we have certain issues in our lives He is there to remind us that He is still God. God allowed Satan to test Job, and Satan believed that he could succeed in destroying Job. Therefore he began the attacks on Job's life, but before he did, Satan replied to God,

> "Have You not made a hedge around him,
> around his household, and around all that
> he has on every side? You have blessed the
> work of his hands, and his possessions have

increased in the land. But now, stretch out
Your hand and touch all that he has, and
he will surely curse You to Your face!"

And the LORD said to Satan, "Behold,
all that he has is in your power; only
do not lay a hand on his person."

So Satan went out from the
presence of the LORD.

—Job 1:10–12

Satan doesn't know our future; therefore he targets our present and haunts us with our past. God knew from the beginning that Satan was a loser. He never won; he was a defeated adversary.

Satan went ahead and attacked Job's livestock first, and then he went and killed all his children. One by one messengers came to Job to deliver the bad news, reporting to him about his great loss. Could it get any worse? The enemy didn't stop there; he approached God for another shot at Job. This time he would strike Job with sores, thinking that Job would curse God.

Satan was wrong concerning Job's motives toward God. He thought that the reason why Job continued to trust and serve God was because he had everything. Have you ever been in a position where you had nothing to worry about? You have good health, you are financially established, and you enjoy other blessings, and then you start limiting yourself on serving God faithfully in the midst of your abundance.

In this case, Job recognized that since he had started serving God things had been much better for him; therefore, there would be no reason for him not to obey God's commands. However, Satan just wanted to prove that Job worshipped God not because he loved Him but because God had given him a life with surplus.

This is how Satan analyses us: he tests our motives to determine how much we trust the God we serve. How deep will your faith take you in believing that God will deliver you through the tempestuous seasons in your life? It's amazing just to read about the conversation God had with Satan regarding Job; this proves to us that God knows what we will go through before we experience it. He is fully aware of every attempt by Satan to bring suffering and difficulty upon us.

God will allow us to suffer for a reason beyond our understanding; He is never surprised when we come before Him with our requests. I personally could not handle Job's trials. We should have knowledge about this; God will not give us more than we can carry. In other words, He will not allow us to go through much more than we can handle.

> No temptation has overtaken you except
> such as is common to man; but God is
> faithful, who will not allow you to be
> tempted beyond what you are able, but with
> the temptation will also make the way of
> escape, that you may be able to bear it.
> —1 Corinthians 10:13

I like the way the Amplified translation relates it to us; it states that "No temptation (regardless of it source) has overtaken or enticed you that is not common to human experience, (nor is any temptation unusual or beyond human resistance); but God is faithful to His word, He is compassionate and trustworthy, and He will not let you be tempted beyond your ability to resist, but along with the temptation, He has in the past and is now and will always provide the way out as well, so that you will be able to endure it without yielding, and will overcome temptation with joy."

Job was not quiet about his grief; in fact he made it quite

obvious to the public. The Bible tells us that he rent his clothes, meaning he ripped his garments and cried out aloud without shame. Job's conduct under the weight of his sorrows was not a performance but a real experience. Considering a man of his rank, he had received messages suddenly; when the full extent of his misery came home to him. He then rose and gave way to the liveliest expression of grief.

He rent his mantle, which also signifies that his heart was filled with sorrow. As Joel 2:13 says: "Rend your heart and not your garments."

He shaved his head, put off every adornment as a symbol of mourning, and lay his forehead on the dust, in deepest submission before God. Grief has its rights, which every Christian should stand by to see fulfilled.

It was already obvious to his friends, neighbors, and probably to the nation by the time he received the news. He was in total distress knowing that he had lost everything he'd had.

Job's situation would give the gossipers a great opportunity to bicker. However, Job was focused on what mattered to him most, the evidence of him being stripped of everything without reason was more than enough for him to stay connected to God. After losing the livestock and his children, he'd thought that was enough, and anyone would have thought so.

Then the enemy got permission from God to strike again, and without hesitation he did just that. This time Satan wanted to disgrace Job to the lowest state, which he did. Job was struck by Satan with sores all over his body; the Bible describes it as from head to toe. He couldn't be identified by the people around him. Job must have wondered to himself, *Why me, Lord? Haven't I been through enough? What's left to be done to thy servant, Lord?*

Just think for a minute: Job initially could have taken his life right then. There was nothing to live for at that point, and the God he served had failed him in every way. But that's what Satan thought Job would be thinking, and he wanted Job to curse God and die. However, Job had a relationship with God. He knew that his God would not curse whatever or whomever he'd blessed. Job knew his source wasn't from man; he knew that the blessings and wealth he'd had were not permanently lost. He also knew that the God he served was a restorer, a way maker, a provider, one who sustained and helped in time of trouble and need.

Therefore, Job had to connect himself to the source, which was the Lord of his life; he knew nothing more. Even though this story is very sad at first, I believe it has a very strong lesson of faith, perseverance, control, faithfulness, endurance—and most of all, the love he had for his Savior.

There was a time in my life when I was at my lowest, and I had no one to assist me in fulfilling my needs. I was depressed, stressed, and tired of the direction my life was heading. I had just started a new job, and it was very demanding. With no time for rest or a vacation, it was work, church, and college. It was so intense, and then one morning when I was getting ready for work I looked in the mirror and discovered that something was wrong with my skin.

There were different sizes of pimples on my neck and arms, with just a couple on my face. I thought to myself, *I've already had the chicken pox, so it can't be that.* I decided to go to work, hoping it would go away soon. After a few hours, I realized that more spots were appearing, and they began to itch. I became worried about what was happening to me. The following morning my body was covered with different sizes of bumps, and they were painful.

I decided to visit the doctor, who did a blood test. A skin specialist examined me to find out what had caused the reaction. The results came, and they told me it was chicken pox. They were baffled because they couldn't pinpoint the actual cause of the breakout. It was worrying for me, as I had no answer as to the reason for the skin rashes. I began praying to God, asking to know the reasons behind the attack I was experiencing.

I started to label it as an attack from the enemy. I felt I needed backup in prayer. I decided to make contact with my bishop, and he came to my house to pray with me. At this point I stayed home, because it was shameful for me to be in public with my condition. When the bishop arrived at my home, he was dumbstruck to see my skin; he could hardly look at me and sat a distance away as he prayed.

I felt scorned and neglected, so my initial thought was, *How must Job have felt when he was tested by the things he went through?* Job went through worse than what I was going through, and even though they could not find the cause of my problem, I was totally healed by God. Although Job's situation was much worse than mine, I couldn't understand why God's servants had to go through pain and struggles. As time went by, I became spiritually mature in Him. I understood process and change and how it only happens so we can become stronger and more equipped in Christ Jesus.

The Bible mentioned three friends that Job had who, when the news reached them about his condition, immediately stopped by to support him. However, in the long run they became very critical of Job while keeping his company. The conversations between Job and his friends became more judgmental on him rather than sincerely supportive. Job had to defend himself and his relationship with God many times, and these three guys seemed determined to bring more pain to Job.

There are certain people who will come into your life for that purpose—to bring joy to you when you need it. And in another situation those same people cannot be helpful to you, because they are not the right ones to help at that time. We cannot be wholly dependent on individuals or family; their instructions and predications might not necessarily be right. The Bible says, "But seek ye first the Kingdom of God and His righteousness, and all these things shall be added to you" (Matt. 6:33). If you seek advice from man, the result could bring you to a place of pain and sorrow.

God expects you to seek Him in good and bad times. When you cannot manage to pay your bills, when you are abused by your spouse, when you are sick, when you don't have family or friends, when you are jobless, when all seems to be failing you, you need to seek God through prayer and meditation. Reach out to him in your quiet time, and become intimate with him through praise and worship. He is waiting for you to approach him. His word said that he will never leave you nor forsake you.

I believe that God is speaking to you now as you read this book and asking you to put aside every weight that so easily besets you. Then press toward the mark of the higher calling, which is in Christ Jesus, even when your back is against the wall, and when your friends fail you, when your family is against you, when you have no strength left, and when it seems as if all hope is lost.

God is waiting, with His arms wide open, to receive you as His child. He wants to comfort you and deliver you from the enemy of your soul. Satan only wants your soul. He wants the glory for himself; he wants you to curse God and die. He has nothing good to offer you but only sin, shame, and open disgrace. Look what he did to Job just to win him over to his path. How can he conduct evil schemes against someone and then expect them to love him? You can now see for yourself that Satan does not care for God's children. He desires to totally destroy them and bring them to where he is, in the pit of hell.

God planned for us to have the best from the time the earth was created. He provided everything that we could desire to have, but because of sin and temptation luring us into the evil ways of the enemy, we became trapped in bad habits and unclean thoughts. These will not only bring us to shame but also pull us away from God. But we know that we are more than conquerors only through Christ Jesus. We cannot fight this battle on our own, and we cannot win this war without the full armor of God.

When we go out on the battlefield, we must be fully equipped, full of his power and might, ready to destroy the kingdom of the enemy. The Bible said, "The kingdom of heaven suffers violence, and the violent we take it by force." We must take back our children by force, our finances, and our spouses (if we want them back). We must also take back our dignity by force; our jobs, our peace and joy, our blessings, and everything that we have lost, we must take back by force. We have the power to do so as we stand upon God's word, which is our sure foundation and our solid rock. Then we must fight with everything we have—continue to fight on, my friends, for the battle is already won, but we can't be complacent at this time in our journey with God.

When Job's wife saw the state of her husband and realized everything had been lost, her faith in God disappeared. She actually pleaded with her husband to curse God and die. The only result that will come after you curse God is death. When she looked at her husband's condition, all she saw was death.

His situation was so bad that she gave up on God, whom she had served faithfully for years in the time of plenty. But now all she could see was hopelessness, death, and disappointment. Then Satan was given the chance to use her to convince Job to curse God and blame Him for what had happened (even though he knew he had something to do with Job's circumstances). The wife's relationship with God seemed unstable; her trust was in the material things and probably her fame. Now a change for the worse had come, and she desired of her husband to accompany her in doubting God. It is obvious now that she had already cursed God in her mind and was beginning to blame Him for their losses.

> A good man out of the good treasure of
> his heart brings forth good; and an evil
> man out of the evil treasure of his heart
> brings forth evil. For out of the abundance
> of the heart his mouth speaks.
>
> —Luke 6:45

She had been thinking of her conclusion to the matter for some time and was able to notify her husband about her thoughts. Even the closest person to you can influence you to curse God. Sometimes it might be the ones you think should be there to hold your hand when you become weak and have no strength to move forward.

There are times when God will remove certain individuals from your life so that you will see where He aspires to lead you. Our spiritual eyes are very important. We need to discern the things around us and the people we associate ourselves with. The Bible asks "That our eyes be enlightened so that we can see and our ears be opened to hear the truth." We need to be alert in the spirit to know and understand what God is saying to us when He is speaking. God relates in different ways to us. He communicates to us in dreams, through His word, and also through His servants.

We should be aware of the devil when he speaks. Job's wife was listening to another voice, which was leading her to her death and was influencing her to deceive Job. But Job was wise enough to understand when God was speaking.

Another example is Adam and Eve in the garden. Eve did not obey the voice of God; she was influenced by the voice of Satan. God speaks through His word. Anything you hear from someone, whether it's something from a prophet or a word of knowledge, must be in line with the word of God. It must also be confirmed to you first. In other words, it must not be the first time you are hearing it.

Job knew his God, and he knew when the messages he heard were from God; this is only because he had a personal relationship with God. He spoke to God daily; therefore, he was familiar with the voice of God when He spoke. The man immediately rebuked his wife for being unwise, for allowing the enemy to use her the way he did. There are people who prefer to listen to what man says rather than God, to take the easier option.

These options can be very tempting if we are not careful;

we need to be equipped and ready in season and out of season, whenever the enemy strikes. The enemy's job is to prowl around the earth and deceive every human being. He is ready to devour and discover who will be his next victim and who will surrender to his tricks. Let us be very aware of the plans of the devil and not let ourselves be his next prey. I pray that you will come to the full knowledge and truth of God, partake of the gospel of Christ Jesus, and depend upon Him in everything, even at your weakest moments.

Struggling emotionally or physically can be deeply painful, and most of the time it will take you to a place of misery. Never underestimate how vulnerable you are during a season of suffering and pain. Always be steadfast to your faith. Do not blame others for your failures and disappointments in life. Whenever misfortunes come along your pathway, your human nature may think that its witchcraft or a curse that is being pronounced over you.

You might be experiencing physical pain right now or even spiritual discomfort. The first step is to pray, trust in God, and wait patiently for His directions. Even if you are placed at a crossroads right now in your faith and believe that God has forgotten you, just rest in his lovely, caring arms—a set of arms that will never fail you in the long run. Pull from the source of God.

What's your real purpose in serving God? Is it to be happy all the time, without pain and suffering? The purpose of life is not just happiness and personal fulfilment but to serve and honor God. The true meaning and worth of life is not based on how or what we feel. In reality, no one can take away God's divine love from us. Let us not be comfortable in assuming that because God loves us He will always prevent suffering from approaching us. God's love for us cannot be limited or measured by how severely or slightly we may suffer or go through rough times.

According to Romans 8:38–39, "For I am persuaded that neither death nor life, nor angels nor principalities nor powers, nor things present nor things to come, nor height nor depth, nor any other created thing, shall be able to separate us from the love of God which is in Christ Jesus our Lord."

Job must have thought the same way while he was going through his sufferings. He must have thought to himself that neither death, nor the loss of his children or livestock, the sores on his skin, the love for his wife, and certainly not his friends could separate him from the love he had for his God. It's as easy as this: God works in all things, not just for incidents that can cause us to be isolated. He does it for our good. This clearly doesn't mean that everything that happens to us should be for our good.

Remember that Satan stalks the children of God, and therefore evil will always present itself. It is prevalent in our world today. Look around you and see what is happening to our world and people. Evil is very present, but God is able in every situation to turn our circumstances around for His good. We don't need to worry; we should begin to pray and trust in God our Lord and Savior. God doesn't owe us anything. He's not doing what He does to make us happy; He does it to fulfill His divine purpose for us, His children.

This purpose is not for all of us because we think we deserve it—it's only for those who love Him and obey His will and are called according to His purpose. Those who are called are the ones whom the Holy Spirit convinced and enabled to receive Jesus Christ.

These people have a new perspective, a new mind-set toward life. They will trust and rely on God—not the things in life that they can easily become attached to or treasure. They look for safety in heaven and in God, not on this earth. They will learn to accept, not reject, pain and persecution, because God is always with them. He's not a man that he should lie. Christ wants us to be like Him.

Beloved, now we are children of God; and it
has not yet been revealed what we shall be, but
we know that when He is revealed, we shall
be like Him, for we shall see Him as He is.

—1 John 3:2

CHAPTER 17

THE END RESULT

We must recognize that our lives are a process of becoming more and more like Christ Jesus and this process will not and cannot be completed until we see the face of our God and King.

> For our citizenship is in heaven, from which
> we also eagerly wait for the Savior, the Lord
> Jesus Christ, who will transform our lowly
> body that it may be conformed to His glorious
> body, according to the working by which He
> is able even to subdue all things to Himself.
> —Philippians 3:20–21

The "lowly" bodies make reference to the present bodies in the grave and receiving the heavenly bodies when we die in Christ. No more shall we struggle with pain, physical limitations, or disabilities; we will have a divine hope that will set us free.

Therefore, as we become more and more like our God, we will discover our true natures, the persons we were created to be. We can only be conformed to God's will by studying His word and life on this earth through the gospel of Jesus. We must be filled with His Spirit by doing the work of God throughout this world.

As believers we need to have direct contact with God, which can occur if we remain in the Spirit and not the flesh. It's important for believers to have the Spirit of God, to enable them to understand the Bible and the mysteries found in His word through their relationship with Him.

The Holy Spirit guides, teaches, directs, and leads the people of God to the right path. When someone becomes a believer, he or she automatically accepts the truth about Jesus Christ: the fact that He came into this world, made an ultimate sacrifice so we would receive life, and then He rose again triumphantly from the grave in order that we receive eternal life.

No one else on the earth could have made that ultimate sacrifice for us, but Jesus did. Simply believing the truth and accepting the confirmation through the word of God will put us on the pathway in the faith and power of His love for us. When we believe in Him, we automatically become His children.

Jesus Christ called us His friends; what an awesome opportunity to become a friend of God. He journeys with us, He listens to us, and He helps us when we are in need. He comforts us when we are down, and He heals us when we are sick. Who could trade such a friend, one who gave up His life for us? Relationship is one of the key elements in serving God. Developing a relationship with God takes discipline, perseverance, holiness, righteousness, faith, and commitment to study His word.

It's basically a daily walk in obedience. Without obeying the will of God, we head in the direction of failure. As disciples of Christ we often fail to follow the commandments of God, especially when we are being attacked by the enemy. Why is it always easy to fight our own battles? Our initial move is often to do things our own way and not God's. The pressures of life will force us to yield first to our fleshly desires and needs and then, when we fail to overcome, our next move is to call on our creator.

It is normally our first call—"Jesus!"—when we are in trouble. Even those who are not Christians and have no personal relationship with Jesus call on His name whenever they are experiencing trouble.

I remember, when I was in London, I one day took a cab because my car had broken down. While I was in the cab, the driver began to talk to me about his day, and the conversation went even further into his personal life. I found out that he was a Muslim. The Islamic religion recognizes Jesus not as their savior but as a prophet.

As he was approaching my destination, a car swerved right beside us and almost hit the side of the cab. Suddenly the driver shouted out, "Jesus!" In a state of shock, I was more surprised to hear him call on the name of Jesus when he was in trouble than I was by the near accident. He didn't call on Allah, but he called on the name of Jesus.

Do unbelievers understand the power in the name of Jesus when they call on Him? And will their call be answered despite the fact that they are not having a relationship with Him?

Unbelievers take the Bible as another book of unexplained words. The Bible will not make sense to them, because they haven't experienced the intimacy of God's love and built a relationship with Him. The unbelievers have not encountered the Holy Spirit, and it will be difficult for them to understand the whole truth that is in the word of God.

God's word works with the inspiration of the Holy Spirit, who guides you through the passages and brings an understanding and revelation of the truth.

Nothing is impossible when you use the word of God effectively. The important thing is to have a positive mind-set coupled with a healthy mind, both spiritually and physically. People who think positively can see potential in even the most discouraging situations, while those who think negatively are quick to point out problems and limitations. This goes beyond the proverbial idea of simply seeing a glass as half-full or half-empty and extends to actually making decisions and taking actions based on either positive or negative thinking.

Have you ever noticed that negative thinking blows things out of proportion? Problems start to seem larger and much more difficult than they really are. Sometimes a problem may actually be impossible for us to handle in the natural. A negative mind-set forgets that nothing is impossible to God. Meditating on God's word will rid you of negativity and help you refocus on who God is. A positive mind-set, based on God's word, means you know that nothing is beyond God; He is always present.

Kingdom principles must be adhered to as you develop positively in the word of God.

> For with God nothing will be impossible.
> —Luke 1:37

You must train your brain to believe God and His word. You will receive the experience and claim the power available to you through God when you trust Him more than your circumstances. You need to always remember that nothing is impossible with God.

The word gives instructions for us to follow; if we don't adhere to it we can easily fall into the trap of the enemy. The children of Israel had a very good reason to believe in God and obey His commands. They'd had great, miraculous experiences right before their eyes. They had also witnessed the demonstration of His power and love on earth, but still they continued to be unfaithful to God. Even though we might experience the dynamic miracles of God, there are times we may find it difficult to obey Him and remain faithful to Him. Hence, we thank God for the Bible, the written records of God's miraculous acts throughout history.

Reading the word of God gives us a panoramic view of both the miracles Israelis saw and the others they didn't see. If we take note of the lessons from the past, the instructions given for our present time and the insight into the future will give us many opportunities to strengthen our faith in God. Deuteronomy 11:18 declares, "Therefore you shall lay up these words of mine in your heart and in your soul, and bind them as a sign on your hand, and they shall be as frontlets between your eyes." In other words, you need to totally depend on the word of God. Live it, breath it, walk with it, talk it, teach it, experience it, and love it.

Another method for allowing the word to work for you is embracing the truth that it delivers. Let it work for you, believe what it says, and act on it; then it will accomplish the purpose it serves. The word will clearly demonstrate His power; that is the requirement, and you cannot embrace what He will do for you until you hold onto what He has done.

It is always easy to dwell on what God says he'll do, and you must move forward believing that the work is accomplished. If you try to accept, and know the things you haven't seen, and hope for the victory in the waiting, you will one day embrace all the things He has done for you through your patience.

The word also will inflict changes in your life and take you to a higher level in the rank of God's servanthood. Because of the various devices available these days, it is easy to be misguided about the truth of the word of God, even though the changes are vitally important.

Why should you change? Only a person who hungers for a higher level can reach it. You live in an information era in which things need to be updated to flow with the movements of the world. New technologies are coming forth, and you may miss out if you fail to adapt to changes. If you don't move with the changes, you will become obsolete in this society.

It takes great courage to push yourself to places that you have never been before. At this minute, just make up your mind, and say: "I'm making a change in my life; my attitude will change for the better. The way I pray will change, and my study of God's word will change."

During your period of waiting for change to occur, nobody will see you, because God will place you in the hiding. Nobody will know the shedding of your tears, and not one person will see your pain. Look at Jabez (I Chronicles 4:9, 10). He asked God to bless him, to enlarge his coast and territory, and God answered him in his time of waiting for change.

Sometimes it takes years of failures and setbacks to become an "immediate success." Abraham Lincoln, for instance, had two failed businesses and one nervous breakdown; he endured the death of his sweetheart and was defeated for public office no less than ten times over the space of almost thirty years. Then, unbelievably, he was elected president of the United States.

Don't be discouraged by repeated setbacks, apparent failures, and personal tragedies that may defeat your vision for the future. These should rather strengthen your character and commitment to move forward. The light of day will finally enter your reformatory life cycle, and the time for which God has prepared you will quickly arrive.

CHAPTER 18

REACHING YOUR WITS' END

A certain woman of the wives of the sons of the prophets cried out to Elisha, saying, "Your servant my husband is dead, and you know that your servant feared the LORD. And the creditor is coming to take my two sons to be his slaves." So Elisha said to her, "What shall I do for you? Tell me, what do you have in the house?" And she said, "Your maidservant has nothing in the house but a jar of oil."

Then he said, "Go, borrow vessels from everywhere, from all your neighbors—empty vessels; do not gather just a few. And when you have come in, you shall shut the door behind you and your sons; then pour it into all those vessels, and set aside the full ones." So she went from him and shut the door behind her and her sons, who brought the vessels to her; and she poured it out. Now it came to pass, when the vessels were full, that she said to her son, "Bring me another vessel." And he said to her, "There is not another vessel." So the oil ceased. Then she came and told the man of God. And he said, "Go, sell the oil and pay your debt; and you and your sons live on the rest."

—2 Kings 4:1–7

Moving on means being satisfied with what you have accomplished, whether it's good or bad. The Father has done many things for us, more than we can imagine. But some things can stop us from being satisfied with what God has offered us.

To list a few, we have greed and we have jealousy over what belongs to someone else when we are trying to meet our own lustful desires. We must pull away and let it go. We must stop holding on to what is not beneficial to us and embrace the one thing that will make a difference in us.

The passage of scripture above describes Elijah and the mantle in a profound way. He wasn't afraid to use what he had. Firstly, he knew the power it had, and he wasted no time. He knew the connecting force of the mantle through God. Find out what your mantle is, and don't be afraid to activate it. Do the best you can with what you have. Change your environment, change your lifestyle, and most of all, change your world.

Elijah also had the fire of God upon him, and therefore the mantle was activated to be used in every situation. "If your mantle is your mouth, ask God to place His fire in it; if it's your hands, to put the fire on them; and if it's your feet, put the fire on them." Our feet signify walking in the pathway of God. We often ask God to direct our steps in His word. We need the fire of God on our feet to walk Holy before Him; faith should be in our feet as we travel on this journey.

If you should desire to have the fire of God in your life, body, marriage, and family, try not to yearn for anything that's not yours. It makes no sense, because what belongs to you is yours. God will bless and increase what He has given to you. Do not try to get God to bless something that is already cursed. God will not curse what He has blessed. Believe this: God has blessed you in abundance—you probably haven't seen it yet, but He has.

We are blessed people whether we know it or not, but here's a question for you. Have you ever been in a situation wherein you felt you had reached the end of the rope in your life? You had no one or nowhere to turn to? Just to let you know, God has another plan set up for you. You are blessed.

The miraculous story above illustrates obedience, trust, commitment, love, favor, and blessings from God. The woman wasn't named, but her situation was highlighted. She was described as the wife of a prophet; therefore we can assume that she knew the blessing of the Lord in her home and both she and her husband had a relationship with God. She carefully explained to Elisha that her husband had died. That Elisha probably knew her husband or knew of him was suggested when she mentioned to him, "Thou know that thy servant did fear the Lord."

Now her situation had changed, and she was left alone with her children. This unknown widow must have been going through some rough times with her neighbor, knowing that she was the wife of a prophet; being a good prophet in those days was very popular. Maybe there was some talk, and the fact that she was in serious debt could have brought more stress on her.

Elisha was the prophet who succeeded Elijah—the one who received the double portion from God and used that power effectively to perform many miracles in his time. So the man of God asked her a question: "What shall I do for you?" and said, "Tell me, what have you got in your house?"

Her answer was straight and to the point: "I only have a pot of oil." Imagine that—the woman was at the end of her rope. All she had was some oil. As we all know, oil by itself cannot comprise a meal to eat.

If we should look at the word *house* that was mentioned earlier, it might mean the physical house for the woman, but for us today it represents a spiritual house. Many of us find our spiritual houses are empty, and we are in desperate need for help. We have lost our first loves, and now we have become empty.

Not even enough substance of the word will sustain us. We

need a refilling, we need restoration, and we need abundant blessings from our Father. God wants to fill us up again, so He is asking us to prepare ourselves for what's about to happen next. There is going to be an outpouring and overflow; therefore we need to get ourselves in position and shut in with the King.

Whatever the man of God, Elisha, said to the widow sounded serious. She might have thought to herself, "How can he ask me to do such a ridiculous thing? I might be desperate but not foolish." You know how we perceive things in our minds before we act! But God knows our thoughts from far off; that's why His mercy, grace, and compassion are always with us. Elisha said, "Go collect some vessels, even borrow some from your neighbors." This is a very important moment for her breakthrough, but even though she was obedient to the prophet, she had no clue as to what was coming next to her house.

Someone, right now—and if that's you, begin to act on your faith and move out of your comfortable dwelling of embarrassment—confront your situation, because it time for your breakthrough. It is time to prepare your spiritual vessel. A vessel is a container, something that can hold or contain something. It's not a utensil or an instrument; a vessel is not used to do something but to contain substance.

> Does not the potter have power over the
> clay, from the same lump to make one vessel
> for honor and another for dishonor?
> —Romans 9:21

We have already been molded and created as vessels of God through the knowledge of the truth of His word. We became empty and dry, with nothing in us, because of the dead situation that had occurred in our lives. We cannot allow the dead situations that occur in our lives to leave us in shame. God is looking for clean vessels to be used in His kingdom. Firstly, God wants to clean us up so that we will be available for usage. There are three things that we need to do before we can be filled with His power and anointing:

1. Be available
2. Be accessible
3. Be at the right location

God wants available vessels; He is searching for those who are willing to be used for His purpose and destiny. You can be present but not available because of distractions around you. Making yourself available means being sensitive to people you come in contact with. You realize that God is orchestrating your life and putting people in your path, from people you encounter casually to those you live and work beside. The more available you make yourself to Him, the more He will use you. This follows the same principle as in Luke 6:38: "Give, and it shall be given to you: good measure, pressed down ..." If you make yourself available to be used by God, He will cause people to cross your path whom He has prepared to hear the Gospel.

To be accessible is to be present with God, by having an intimate connection with Him when you find yourself available. Intimacy is what we call the experience of really knowing and being known by another person or the Creator.

We frequently use spatial language when describing this experience. An intimate friend is someone we feel very *close* to; he or she knows us at a *deep* level. If something happens that damages the intimacy with our friend, he or she feels *distant* from us. Or a person who doesn't know us intimately knows us at a *superficial* level. He wants to have He wants to have a deeper relationship with us in order to know and experience His power in our lives.

To be at the right location with God can be difficult when

you are distracted by situations around you. When you are at the right location, He requires your attention, because He already knows your circumstances. God is never taken by surprise when it comes to you and your future. He has preplanned your life. He has already made preparations for your success and victory regarding everything that concerns you—including whatever problems, struggles, or uncertainties may be holding you back.

Every day He is providing you with God moments—opportunities to exercise your faith and watch seemingly impossible situations become possible. He's giving you opportunities in different, exciting ways, through people, places, or things that are perfectly suited for you. You will be ushered through open doors into your new season of blessings, success, prosperity, and victory.

Just like the potter and the clay, when you are broken and out of use, God is always there to pick up the pieces and mend you again. However, the important process is to be available to God, to be accessible in His presence and to ensure you are at the right location to begin the process.

God's hands are ready and waiting to work on you, through the wheeling and the spinning process. He will not commence the work until you become what He has destined for you; He is shaping you to become the best. Be ready for what's about to happen with you.

"Arise and go down to the potter's house,
and there I will cause you to hear My words."
Then I went down to the potter's house,
and there he was, making something at
the wheel. And the vessel that he made of
clay was marred in the hand of the potter;
so he made it again into another vessel, as
it seemed good to the potter to make.
—Jeremiah 18:2–4

The Bible says that the woman mentioned to the man of God, Elijah, that after her husband had passed everything had turned upside down. To that effect, her creditors were demanding for children to be used as payments of her debt.

Your enemy might tell you that it is all over for you, you have nothing left, and you might as well give up and die. But the devil is a thief and a liar. There is hope for you. Don't believe his lie that your circumstances cannot change. There is hope for you as long as you are walking in God's will. Establish yourself in His word, and prepare to be filled so that you can be used and live again.

Your brightest days are ahead of you; the sun will shine again. Your spiritual house might be empty, but your answer is on its way. The Bible says that the woman went immediately for those vessels, because she was desperate and needed a miracle. She borrowed all that she could and shut herself in. When God is about to pour into you, it would be wise to begin shutting yourself away from the crowd—the neighbors, the critics, and even some family members. Until the oil stops flowing, just focus on what God is doing in you. The oil here represents the anointing of God.

> It shall come to pass in that day
> That his burden will be taken
> away from your shoulder,
> And his yoke from your neck,
> And the yoke will be destroyed
> because of the anointing oil.
> —*Isaiah 10:27*

When the anointing starts to pour out in our vessels, yokes will be broken, and things will never be the same again. We will begin to walk in abundance, without the burden of loss and lacking and with no more yokes around our necks. We will be free to walk in His purpose. Our households will be blessed; our children will be freed. We will be filled to overflowing so that we may go and tell others about the goodness of Jesus, and they will be impacted by the power of the anointing of God. God's supplies for us can be as large as our faith and obedience in Him. We cannot limit our faith at this point, since believing is the key to success.

The lesson learned here was that the woman in her pain and poverty did only the thing that she knew she could do. She turned to the Lord, and when she did that, God honored His word and came through for her in a very big way. The passage also teaches us the glorious truth that God has a plan for our problems. Just as God took care of the widow, he will take care of all of us. Whenever we reach the ends of our ropes, there is help and there is hope waiting for us.

We must not give up when faced with questions such as, "What do I do when I'm confronted with troubles with my children that I cannot solve?" or "What I do when my marriage is on the rocks and unrelenting waves of hopelessness are crushing me?" or "What do I do when there are problems at work and it seems that there is no way of escape?"

It may be that you have lost a family member and you cannot get over the pain and grief. Or you may be experiencing a broken heart because of a bad relationship. Your dreams have been shattered and your hopes smashed to bits on the cruel rocks of reality.

What do you do when you are walking through a spiritual wasteland and there seems to be no way out? There have been so many questions, but for sure it's only the good Lord who can answer them for us. All we must do at this point is prepare our vessels for the Lord. The preparation might be difficult for some of us; however, we cannot give up hope in trying and pushing our way toward our victory line. There the answer awaits us, accompanied by great joy and peace from the heavenly Father.

CHAPTER 19

GOD KNOWS OUR PREDICAMENTS

The word *predicament* can be described as a difficult, unpleasant, or embarrassing circumstance. God knows when you are in one of those low places in your life that requires His help. People express themselves through crying, a sign of despair. They may be mourning or weeping uncontrollably to shrink themselves out of grief, emphasizing the sound of a broken heart. There are many broken women who are weeping about their conditions, women who are distressed and will do anything possible to be released from their pain.

I was at a place in my life where pain was as solid as a block of ice. It was a place where tears had become my comfort—the solution to ease the damaging feelings that were self-inflicted. We can be our worst enemies during a time of depression or oppression. We tend to cage everything in and cushion the pain, not knowing the implications it might have in the future.

I was rescued from my pain when I decided one day to talk to God out loud and express my deepest feelings, even though He already knew what was confronting me and the end result of the struggles. I told God everything: the secrets, the mistakes, and the pain, and then I emptied my heart to him. I became that empty vessel God wanted to use. One of my favorite Psalms is 121; this talks about where our help comes from. Here is the first verse:

I will lift up my eyes to the hills—
From whence comes my help?
—Psalm 121:1

That was all I did—I looked up to the hills. I looked up to my Savior: my source, my helper, my keeper, and my provider. We all need help. We all have problems in our lives, and we all have a deliverer who has promised to honor His word when we call upon him.

Despite what you are going through, hold firm to the grip of faith. If you need help, do not look to family or friends or even try to find someone to help you. Just look to the hills, where your help comes from. When you reach that point in your life where the troubling days and trying times are overwhelming, it may be that the world, the flesh, and the devil are all working together to tell you that God doesn't see and hear you and He doesn't care about your feelings.

The fact is that He does see. He sees everything you are experiencing; not a single thing is hidden from His view, and He does care. He cares more than you know about the situations you are going through. Bearing your doubts, stresses, and daily struggles by yourself shows that you have not trusted God fully with your life. It takes self-effacement, however, to recognize that God cares, to admit your need, and to let others in God's family help you.

Sometimes we think that struggles caused by our sin and foolishness are not God's concern. But when we turn to God in repentance, He will bear the burden of even those struggles. We should allow God to have our worries; this calls for action, not passivity. Don't submit to conditions of your life but to the Lord who controls circumstances.

Casting all your care upon Him,
for He cares for you.

—1 Peter 5:7

The verse above is intended to teach us that our problems, which may appear to be insurmountable before our eyes, are really just God's opportunities in disguise. Therefore, no matter what you are called to face in this life, learn to turn to the Lord first for the help that is needed. He cares! He is able! He will work on your need.

God knows our deepest thoughts, even from far off. He sympathizes with our griefs and pain, and He is certainly not cold and unfeeling toward our desires. We have one who is abundantly qualified to sympathize with us in our afflictions, and therefore we should look for aid and support in all trials. If we had a high priest who was cold and heartless, who simply performed the external duties of his office without sympathy toward those who came to seek pardon, who had never experienced any trials, and who felt himself above those who sought his aid, then we would definitely feel disheartened and discouraged.

Such coldness would repel us. His pomposity, distance, and reserve would keep us away and perhaps render us indifferent to every desire to be saved. But sensitivity and sympathy attract those who are delicate, and kindness does more than anything else to encourage those who have to encounter difficulties and dangers.

Jesus went through the pain and suffering such as we encounter at present—and even worse. He is like us: He experienced a full range of temptations throughout His life as a man. Thanks be to God! We can be encouraged in knowing that Jesus faced temptation without giving in to sin; it's sometimes hard but we can do it. He shows us that we do not have to sin when facing the seductive lure of temptation. Jesus is the only perfect human being who ever lived, and He knows exactly what we are going through.

For we do not have a High Priest who cannot
sympathize with our weaknesses, but was in
all points tempted as we are, yet without sin.
—Hebrews 4:15

God will sometimes allow our situations to be broadcast
publicly. He will cause things to happen to us for which we need
to consult a neighbor or friend.

God requires of us to be witnesses, and what witnesses we
will be when He encounters our need! God will use our living,
breathing situations to bring sermons to our neighbors or friends.
He does the same thing to all of us. We often talk about how
we love God; at times it's just words, until we face the valley
experience, being in that place where we are shut in. When we are
there, and He delivers us in an elaborate way, it speaks volumes to
those who are watching.

It's so amazing, because we never know who the Lord will use
in our lives to speak to us. We must allow God to have His way in
us. Now we have become life's billboard for advertising the grace,
blessings, and power of God to a lost and dying world.

For we are His workmanship, created in Christ
Jesus for good works, which God prepared
beforehand that we should walk in them.
—Ephesians 2:10

In the believer's life cycle, most of us would want to always
enjoy the mountain experience (Matthew 17:4). "Then Peter
answered and said to Jesus, "Lord, it is good for us to be here."
You do not transfer from one mountain to the other without going
through the valleys. Many people are bound in spiritual prisons or
physically incarcerated; they have given up hope of reaching the

top, because they see themselves stigmatized by society as a result of their imprisonment.

There is a way of escape. Our God will take the evil out of men and use the life situation for our good and for His glory. The outworking of God's purpose for all of our lives is seen in Romans 8:28: "And we know that all things work together for good to those who love God, to those who are the called according to His purpose."

We are required to be ready at all times to work for our creator, to demonstrate His good works wherever we go and whatever we do. The moment we experience the evidence of God manifesting His power through us and the witnessing of others, we must begin to act accordingly. He calls for us to be clothed in a place of dependence; then His people will see Him come through for them time after time. This was the experience Elijah had in 1 Kings 17, another great story to reflect on.

As well, consider Daniel 6, the experience with Daniel when he was thrown into the lion's den. The only one he depended on was his God, whom he prayed to night and day—the very God he was forbidden to pray to. Another story of depending only on God is told in Daniel 3, this time involving Shadrach, Meshach, and Abednego. It is a well-known story that has blessed many lives even to this very day.

They were thrown into a fiery furnace because they refused to bow down to other gods. They declined to settle for less; they had a relationship with their God that was second to none. It was a relationship in which trust and faith were at the highest peak in their lives. There are many more related stories in the Bible that could illustrate the power of totally depending on God to deliver us out of our predicaments. Just to list a couple more, there is the one of the five thousand people who were fed with five loaves and two fish, which is cited in John 6, and the one relating the experience of the disciples on the stormy Sea of Galilee, from Mark 6.

Whenever the Lord delivers His people, the work He does might be widely known, but the greatest work is in the hearts of His children. When the Lord moves in His power, His children receive a lesson in faith that can never be taken away from them. Their faith will be expanded, and they will never be the same again. Paul wrote of his experience, saying, "Who art Thou, my Lord?"

> And he said, "Who are You, Lord?"
> Then the Lord said, "I am Jesus, whom
> you are persecuting. It is hard for
> you to kick against the goads."
> —Acts 9:5

Now, since Jesus had met Paul and delivered him, Paul then said,

> Now to Him who is able to do exceedingly
> abundantly above all that we ask or think,
> according to the power that works in us, to
> Him be glory in the church by Christ Jesus
> to all generations, forever and ever. Amen.
> —Ephesians 3:20–21

The difference here is that Paul's faith had been expanded on numerous occasions by the trials of his life and the powerful movement of God. This is what the Lord is doing in this season of our lives today. He is also making a lot of impossible situations possible. Do you have an impossible situation? Let me introduce you to the God who can change the impossible to the possible.

CHAPTER 20

A Place of Total Dependence

> But without faith it is impossible to please
> Him, for he who comes to God must
> believe that He is, and that He is a rewarder
> of those who diligently seek Him.
> —Hebrews 11:6

When God shuts us up in a place of total reliance, we will see Him come through for us time after time when we obey and be faithful to His commands.

This story is about the widow of Zarephath and the prophet Elijah. God foretold to Elijah of a famine that was about to take place within the area of his travels. The Lord said He would send a raven to feed him during certain parts of his journey, and God's word came through for the man of God.

God provided water from a brook and bread, which was delivered by a raven to sustain him. Can you imagine the great things God will do for you if you only believe and trust His word? Later, the Bible says it was discovered that the brook had dried up because there was no rain. But God continued to make provision for Elijah and directed him to the widow at Zarephath (1 Kings 17:7–14).

Interestingly, this is how and where God instructed Elijah to move; for the next trip for him was to go and stay at this widow's house. The Bible shares many stories on widows and women with issues in their lives; many of these stories are found in the Old Testament. When Elijah went to the town and saw a woman picking up sticks, immediately he recognized that this was the woman who would provide food for him.

God provides for us in ways that go beyond our imagination, definition, and expectations; He gives us help when we least expect it. No matter how extreme our trials are or how seemingly hopeless our situations, we must look to God for His outstretched hands. Sometimes the greatest miracles can happen to us in the strangest places.

The woman in question was gathering sticks for her last meal with her son when a stranger approached her with a shocking question. We should always be prepared for the unknown. There are angels of God who catch us unawares, and at times we selfishly refrain from doing what is required and miss out on our blessings. The prophet kindly asked the woman to get him some water. Remember that the water brook was dried up and they hadn't experienced any rain for some time.

This woman might have had just one jar of water at her house, enough for herself and her son. But she went to get the water without hesitation, and Elijah beckoned to her to bring some bread while she was getting it. This time the woman answered, "I don't have any bread, but only a handful of flour in a jar, and a little oil, just enough to sustain my family."

The man of God insisted that she go and make him a cake first—and some also for her family. Really! Hadn't he heard her the first time? He not only told her to get the cake for him but also mentioned to her that it was what the God of Israel had instructed.

The woman changed her mind and acted quickly when she

heard him speak of the God of Israel. She must have heard of and experienced the God of Israel in her life; therefore, with faith she accepted the request.

This woman thought she was preparing for her last meal, but then suddenly God came to her aid. She was obedient, going ahead and preparing food for the prophet as instructed. A simple act of faith produced a great miracle. She trusted the prophet Elijah and gave him the last food she had for herself and her son.

Faith is the ultimate step between promise and assurance. God's servant promised her that He would give her more than what she had offered, and without assurance, she believed instantly. Thus by faith it was granted to her. If our faith wavers, a miracle will seem so hard to achieve. Every miracle, big or small, starts with an act of faith; it moves out of what has become the norm and into what you secure by your actions.

There are many insights into the story of the widow of Zarephath. Firstly, God often uses unlikely people and sources to accomplish His purpose. Secondly, God's mercy extends to all people. Regardless of race or socio-economic factors or whether bonded or free, you can be blessed by faith. And lastly, God requires faith, and mark this—the widow's miracle only came after she had prepared a meal for Elijah. It did not come before, not when she started, but after. God did this to teach us how to exercise our faith and act on something that seems impossible. She acted and she saw a great result.

God assures us through His word that all who honestly seek Him and who act in faith based on the knowledge of Him that they possess will be rewarded. It is important to share the gospel of Jesus Christ with others, encourage them to be honest about their life situations, and be diligent in searching for the truth. Those who hear the gospel are responsible for what they have heard; it takes an act of faith to believe it.

Many times born-again believers toss aside God's message that was given to them; sometimes this happens only because of bad experiences with false teachers and preachers of the gospel who taught a different doctrine from God's word.

The answers to our difficulties must be sought from God's revealed truth and His truth only, not from any other source. The empty answers of false teachers are invalid. They do not have the necessary power to address true spiritual needs or to answer the burning spiritual questions of the human heart. Until we are willing to accept the authority of God's truth in our lives, we will not have the answers we need for the things that trouble our hearts and minds and be able to move forward in this world.

There are sermons written without the wisdom and clarity of God's word, and there are messages based on hearsay, which falsely define the truth of God's word.

Beware of false prophets who say they have a message from God for you; anything God says to you is always confirmed by His word. People go around with ears just twitching to receive lies. God's word is not a get-rich-quick scheme or a system to own the biggest house or to drive the most prestigious cars. His word is meant to educate, instruct, correct, direct, and save.

> The entrance of Your words gives light;
> It gives understanding to the simple.
> —Psalm 119:130

When the word of God comes to you, by whatever channel God sends it, it is supposed to bring forth light to your situation, not condemnation or confusion. Even a child should be able to comprehend the word when it's delivered to him or her.

Ephesians 3:1–5 explains how Apostle Paul was given the message of God to be delivered to the Gentiles. The Bible says he was entrusted. In other words, God could rely on him to deliver the truth of the word to His people without changing it to satisfy his own needs. Paul describes himself as a prisoner of Jesus Christ, one who was captured by God to do His will.

You can study the history of Paul's life and see where God called him from. He was a persecutor of the church, who wanted all Christians dead. God met him and turned his life around. Paul then became a messenger for Christ, delivering His undiluted word to His people. Ephesians 3:3 talks about a mystery which Paul said was revealed to him by God. This does not mean something mysterious or spooky in the way of the modern language we use but rather something that was unknown until it was revealed.

Have you ever heard of something so unreal that your mind cannot comprehend it until it's been revealed to you, perhaps by the Holy Spirit or a servant of God, and then it all makes sense? That is how Paul speaks to us through the scriptures, which were given to him as a mystery of Christ.

Have you ever read the Old Testament and felt confused about what you have read? Yes, mystery was not revealed as much in the Old Testament as in the New Testament. Christ has made a difference to us through the revelations in the scriptures. Now we can understand the mystery of God as we welcome the Holy Spirit into our lives to transform us and bring us to a place of truth and grace. We don't always have to depend on someone to deliver a message telling us what to do. We now have the Holy Spirit. The purpose of Christ coming to this earth was that we could have access to the Spirit of God, who saves, heals, delivers, and sets free.

Christ's death and burial might sound mysterious to the unbeliever, but He died so that we could have eternal life with Him. We need to be ambassadors of Jesus Christ, to make all men see the fellowship of the mystery that from the beginning of the world has been hidden in God. This has been God's doing from the beginning, to make available to all mankind the hope of the Messiah (Jesus Christ). He would come to preach, teach, work miracles, and become a missionary to all. By His ministry, He would bring angelic beings to see the wisdom of God in His plan for the Church, which is His people.

With all that Christ did for us, we now can feel boldness and confidence of access to the throne of God. By the faith we have in him we can make direct contact to God through His son, Jesus, asking Him for whatever we need. There is no limit to what God can do; there is no boundary to where He will take us.

We have the power of God in our lives. Now it's up to us to use what He has given us. If we need strength, we can find it in Him; if we need healing, it's in Him; if we need breakthroughs in certain areas of our lives, Christ can give these to us.

As He strengthens us by His Spirit, in our hearts we believe through faith in His word, knowing that we are rooted and grounded in His love. We are able to understand with each other the length, width, height, and depth of His love and can fully experience that amazing, endless love. This will enable us to know practically, through personal experience, the love of Christ, which far surpasses knowledge. We may have that richest experience of being filled by His presence in our hearts—completely filled and flooded with God (Ephesians 3). *Wow!*

The kind of experience you have when you know Christ is priceless; there is no substitution. I invite you today to draw closer to God and pull from Him everything you need. He is available to the lonely, the messed up, the weak, and the helpless. If you feel that life is unfair with you and you're at a point of giving up, I'm here to tell you that you can rise again. Your situation can and will turn around. Let God into your heart now, and watch Him move. Ask Christ to strengthen your heart if you are weak in faith; ask him as David did:

> Create in me a clean heart, O God,
> And renew a steadfast spirit within me.
> Do not cast me away from Your presence,

And do not take Your Holy Spirit from me.
Restore to me the joy of Your salvation,
And uphold me by Your generous Spirit.
—Psalm 51:10–12

We all need the Holy Spirit to sustain us right at this moment, to prevent us from falling back into our sinful lifestyles and habits that are contrary to God's will and purpose for us.

Whether you are a believer or not, as you are reading this book—which is truly from my heart and the heart of God—at this instant, pause and ask God to search you thoroughly and know your heart. Ask Him to try you and test you for any blemishes, anxiety, or evil thoughts. Furthermore, if you possess any wicked or hurtful ways, ask Him and let Him lead you in the path of restoration. This is the way to freedom from hurt, pain, abuse, and loneliness, as God leads us in His pathway, where we can find peace.

As you conclude this book, I pray that you will take serious note of how it has taken you through the word of God and some true stories of Him delivering His children from predicaments of sin, shame, and disgrace. He has demonstrated His healing power in the lives of so many individuals.

God's desire is to do the same for you. Just open up your heart to Him, be honest about your inner feelings toward him, and remove the mask that may have kept you hidden in secret sin and shame.

We may not have all the answers we need in our social capacity. However, what is beyond our human reasoning is not beyond the knowledge of all-knowing God, our supreme being. Remember this: your dreams will be established and will be achieved because God is God and there is none like Him. He is in control and will do what He says; He's not a man that He should lie.

Yes, He is the One who is the beginning and the end of all things, the first and the last. He is God Himself; right now He is announcing to you that He is making everything new for you. Change is coming your way without delay and setback. You must be ready for it! "Behold, the former things have come to pass, and new things I declare; before they spring forth I tell you of them" (Isaiah 42:9).

When you enquire of God's kingdom, you will enjoy the Lord, and you can enjoy whatever work and wealth He gives you as fringe benefits. Do not lose out now—stick to the winning route!

Remember that the Lord, who was with Hannah and the other women mentioned in this book, is also with you at all times, in all circumstances and situations. That is all the more reason why you need to stay close to Him at all times. He will never fail you—never!

Isaiah 43:2 tells us, "When you pass through the waters, I *will be* with you; and through the rivers, they shall not overflow you. When you walk through the fire, you shall not be burned, nor shall the flame scorch you."

You are called by God. There is something great in you, more than you could imagine. You are a carrier of greatness. You are called to build from underneath; people will not see what you are doing for God and what He has planted in you.

God Himself is building you for a purpose, to encourage and develop someone in the word. It's time to embrace the truth about who you are and what God has designed for you. Do not settle for less—aim high! Come out of your box of comfort, out of the precinct of oppression and depression, the zone of discouragement, the zone of loneliness and self-pity, of suicidal thoughts and death. God's arms are open wide now to encircle you, to welcome you into His arms of peace.

When was the last time you felt peace? If it has been a long time since, right now God is waiting for you to surrender your will and your ways to him. Do not feel condemned, because His word (Romans 8:1) says, "*There is* therefore now no condemnation to those who are in Christ Jesus, who do not walk according to the flesh, but according to the Spirit."

The spirit of God is your guide from today forth as you receive your breakthrough. I will conclude this book with a prayer of repentance and deliverance. May God richly bless you, and may your pathway be straight with Him.

Dear God, our Lord and our Savior, today we come to You surrendering all the things that we have held hostage in our lives and which have been torturing us for many years. Lord, please forgive us this day and let Your words penetrate through our lives, that we might be transformed to Your will. May our hearts be cleansed from any secret sins.

We ask you, God, through your son, Jesus Christ, to deliver us from the enemy of sickness and disease, from oppression and depression, from hurts and pains, from marital abuse and physical abuse. Set us free, Lord God, from the evil one who desires to see us perish, who wants us destroyed.

Rescue us, dear Lord, I pray, and bring us to your throne, where we can find you again in our lives and accept you as our Lord and Savior. We know that you will come through for us when we ask in your name. In the name of Jesus Christ, our Lord and Savior, we pray. Amen.

If you are not saved and you now believe in the Lord Jesus Christ as your Savior, just ask Him right now to come into your heart as you repent of your sins. Maybe you are not living the way you should live for Jesus and you would like to come back to Jesus, or maybe you've hurt Jesus today and you want to say you're sorry and tell Him that you love Him. Pray this prayer (say it with all your heart, and confess it with your mouth). Repeat this out loud:

"Lord Jesus, I'm a sinner; I ask you to forgive me of all my sins. I confess my sins before You this day. I rebuke Satan and all his works. I confess that You, Jesus, are the Lord of my life. Thank you, Jesus, for saving me and bringing me to a place of freedom. From this day forward, Lord Jesus, I will be sensitive to how You feel. I won't hurt You anymore; I will obey you. Lord Jesus, I ask you to present me to God the Father in Your name.

Lord Jesus, I believe with my heart and confess with my mouth that you rose from the dead so that I could be saved. I receive you today with all my heart, one hundred percent. Make me a light in a dark place, and from this day forward I will share you with everyone I meet and everyone I know. Jesus, I commit to getting this world for You through the power You instill in me today."

All you need to do now is to believe that you are saved and begin to follow Jesus Christ. Find a place of worship where God's word is truly preached and taught. Ask the Holy Spirit to guide you; He is waiting for you this moment.

"The LORD bless you and keep you; the LORD make His face shine upon you, and be gracious to you; The LORD lift up His countenance upon you, and give you peace" (Numbers 6:24–26). This blessing in Numbers has been spoken in the Church throughout the ages as a declaration over the people. The power in this blessing is that it is in the heart of God to bless us and be gracious toward us. When we seek His face, it glows, because we are His dearly loved children (Romans 8:14–17).

"For as many as are led by the Spirit of God, these are sons of God. For you did not receive the spirit of bondage again to fear, but you received the Spirit of adoption by whom we cry out, 'Abba, Father.' The Spirit Himself bears witness with our spirit that we are children of God, and if children, then heirs—heirs of God and joint heirs with Christ, if indeed we suffer with *Him*, that we may also be glorified together" (Romans 8:14–17).

May God richly bless you.

Printed in the United States
By Bookmasters